GUIDE TO
JOURNALISM

SUSIE BONIFACE

© Haynes Publishing 2019
Published March 2019

A CIP Catalogue record for this book
is available from the British Library.

ISBN: 978 1 78521 580 3 (print)
      978 1 78521 625 1 (eBook)

Library of Congress control no. 2018967377

Published by Haynes Publishing,
Sparkford, Yeovil, Somerset BA22 7JJ, UK.
Tel: 01963 440635
Int. tel: +44 1963 440635
Website: www.haynes.com

Printed in Malaysia.

Series Editor: David Allsop.
Front cover illustration by Alan Capel.

CONTENTS

'A journalist is a reporter out of a job'

Mark Twain

THE FOURTH ESTATE

Put this book down and walk away. The chances are you aren't up to being part of the 'Fourth Estate*', or even pretending that you are. Not because journalism is particularly difficult, but because it requires enough braggadocio and bluster to make Donald Trump blush.

It is possible to bluff one's way through discussions on wine, or Brexit, or even the offside rule, with a little knowledge and some brass neck. But anyone who tries to pull the wool over the eyes of a journalist will be attempting The Greatest Bluff Known To Humankind, because journalists can smell a lie from 500 miles away down a patchy telephone line, while drunk and at closing time. To pull it off, you will need the native cunning of Machiavelli, the coolness of Dean Martin and the same lack of scruples as Del Boy Trotter. You will also need this book.

* *"There are three estates in Parliament; but, in the Reporters' Gallery yonder, there sits a Fourth Estate more important far than they all."* Edmund Burke, 1787, attrib.

If you are still reading, it's because you like a challenge and are by nature persistent. And, probably, because you are impressed by highly-skilled drunks. Which means you have exactly what it takes to be a successful hack.

This book will tell you how to bluff your way into journalism, bluff your way through it and bluff your way out again. And the first thing you need to know is that anyone who says they're a journalist probably isn't.

'Journalist' is a catch-all name for anyone whose work is published in a journal. It can cover everyone from the editor to the crossword compiler, by way of the Green Ink Brigade to the foreign correspondent and a computer producing automated match reports in Newport Pagnell.

These days, anyone with a blog or a YouTube channel can call themselves a journalist, which means that the trade is slightly less exclusive than a public sewer. For a brief period, former *Apprentice* resignee Katie Hopkins claimed to be one in national media, before being consigned to the u-bend of the internet. Even the mainstream has celebrity columnists, editors-at-large and risible correspondents who are to most journalists as a baby lamb is to a kebab shop – significantly less experienced.

Which is why, when a journalist introduces themselves, they tell you their ACTUAL job – such as reporter, photographer, sub-editor, web editor, feature writer, sports pundit or showbiz columnist.

The next thing they will probably do is duck. Because the usual reaction to a journalist saying 'hello' ranges from mild cursing to physical violence, and in extreme cases, death. According to the International Federation of Journalists, 82 journalists and media staff were killed in 2017, most of them deliberately targeted for writing things down.

So why, when the costs of journalism can be so high, does anyone still do it?

Well, because it's the most fun you can have typing. It is still regarded, with occasional accuracy, as glamorous and adventurous. The rubbish part of the job is more than outweighed by the chance to make Prime Ministers panic. Perhaps once a year you get a herogram from the editor, and maybe once in a lifetime you can change the world and win an award for it.

When you're a journalist you get to see behind the curtain, irritate all the right people, enjoy the thrill of regular travel even if it is only to Hull on a Monday night, and drink on expenses.

This short but definitive guide is primarily about print media in the UK, but many of the core principles – or lack thereof – are the same in all sorts of journalism throughout the world, whether it's print, online or broadcast. It will conduct you through the main danger zones often encountered therein, from libel to assault by way of gymkhana reports and Freedom of Disinformation, to the giddy heights of meaningless industry prizes and how not to die drunk on a doorstep. But it will do more. It will provide you with the tools to impress legions of marvelling listeners with your knowledge and insight – without anyone discovering that, before reading it, you didn't know the difference between a banging out and a deathknock.

'Journalism is just organised gossip'

Edward Egglestone

START AT THE BEGINNING

Never begin a bluff without placing it on firm foundations. Journalism is a transient business so the only thing that truly impresses are stories that last forever.

It's why the names Woodward and Bernstein are still uttered with awe, half a century after they brought down a president. It's why awards are sought-after, because they prove at least the judges read it. And it's why, if you want to talk your way into journalism, you first have to talk your way into Fleet Street.

Today this road in London EC4 is filled with coffee shops, lawyers and bankers. The once-glorious edifices of newspaper giants are shabby brick and metal sheds now used for something more profitable, like selling egg sandwiches.

But a good bluffer knows the River Fleet that flows beneath the street once ran black with ink and corpses. It rises as two freshwater streams on Hampstead Heath, but in the past London was so foul that by the time the river reached the Thames it was effectively a sewer. During the

Great Fire of London in 1666 people tried to put out the flames with buckets filled in the Fleet; they contained so little actual water it burned anyway. Considering the river's contents, it may have been an accelerant.

In 1710 Jonathan Swift described the Fleet as filled with: *"Sweepings from Butchers Stalls, Dung, Guts and Blood; Drown'd Puppies, stinking Sprats, all drench'd in Mud; Dead Cats and Turnip-Tops come tumbling down the Flood".* And in 1728 Alexander Pope referred to it as *'Fleet-ditch'* with a *'large tribute of dead dogs'*.

It was the natural spot for the fetid craft of journalism to be born.

STREET OF SHAME

Fleet Street was in what journalists call 'a newsy patch', an area where stories just happen. It was surrounded by the type of people your mother avoids but a journalist adores – slum-dwellers, hookers, Newgate Prison inmates, the merchants of the City of London, the priests at St Paul's Cathedral, the barristers of the Inner Temple and the hanging judges of the Old Bailey.

It was impossible to walk down the road without stepping in news. If as the American historian Edward Egglestone *said 'journalism is just organised gossip'*, Fleet Street was smack bang in the place where you would find most of it.

So it was that on March 11, 1702, in a room next to the White Hart pub close to what was then Fleet Bridge and is now a tarmacked intersection, the first newspaper was printed.

Well, not quite. The business of publishing had operated there since around 1500 when William Caxton's apprentice, the improbably-but-accurately named Wynkyn de Worde, set up shop in a side street. Printing things so just anyone could read them was socially unacceptable, and an invitation to trouble-making. They printed books, plays, legal papers, and political pamphlets that were both incendiary and complete fabrications.

The medieval practice of state censorship ceased in 1641, and almost 300 publications flowered. Few were what might be called a newspaper, and most were considered so chaotic, treasonous or downright false that in 1643 Parliament reintroduced censorship, issuing licenses to approved printers, destroying books, and jailing writers.

BLUFFER'S TIP: *When discussing state regulation, quote the first repudiation of it by poet John Milton in his Areopagitica of 1644: "If we think to regulat Printing, thereby to rectifie manners, we must regulat all recreations and pastimes, all that is delightful, to Man."*

EARLY REGULATION

A dislike of the press doesn't stop politicians using it. Throughout the English Civil War, there were 'reports' of fighting that were little more than fiction. Roundheads and Cavaliers both declared victory at the Battle of Naseby in 1645, confusing both The Reader and modern historians.

After his Restoration, King Charles II tightened rules even further. The only licensed newspaper was the London Gazette, first printed in 1665 and still the official journal for government business. It is slightly less interesting than the paper it is printed on.

Responsibility for enforcement was given to the ancient guild of the Stationers' Company, in return for a monopoly on printing. Fleet Street is filled with alleyways called 'courts', and the 'Stationers' Men' would lurk at the entrances to seize unlicensed news before it hit the streets.

These early journalists – being brilliant bluffers – would send bundles of junk paper out the front door to confuse the heavies, and send the genuine articles out the back. News always finds a way.

The Press could not be controlled, the rich and famous fell back on the laws of libel, and in 1695 Parliament refused to renew the licensing act.

Pamphleting gained in popularity, and in 1701 Daniel Defoe, author of Robinson Crusoe, used such a publication to demand the release of political prisoners – the first journalistic campaign.

But what happened in 1702 was the first time something *recognisable* as a newspaper was printed. The *Daily Courant* consisted of a single page of news from around the world, with adverts on the back. Its aim was to cover news impartially, with sources clearly stated. In the first edition the unknown Editor wrote:

"The Author has taken Care to be duly furnish'd with all that comes from Abroad in any Language... he will not, under pretence of having Private Intelligence... take upon

him to give any Comments or Conjectures of his own, but will relate only Matter of Fact; supposing other People to have Sense enough to make Reflections for themselves."

The good bluffer will know this is the first-ever editorial promise, and a very good bluffer will say that clause 1 of the current Editor's Code of Conduct says much the same: "The Press must take care not to publish inaccurate, misleading or distorted information or images."

An exceptional bluffer will add that the *Daily Courant* was published by a woman named Elizabeth Mallet, which puts claims of Fleet Street's institutional sexism into context, and that as she sold it just 40 days later she was also the first to decide journalism had no future.

THE FLEET STREET PARADIGM

Since then Fleet Street has continued to have a profound influence on journalism around the world. Newspapers, TV stations and websites everywhere still use the *Daily Courant's* model, guaranteeing independence with advertising, pledging to tell the truth, and pretending they think the audience is clever enough to spot fake news.

BLUFFER'S TIP: *Fleet Street is not to be confused with Grub Street, a similarly seedy road in the Moorfields district of London, whose dosshouses, brothels and garrets were home to aspiring writers, novelists and poets. They called it 'bohemian'; but as noted in Samuel Johnson's Dictionary, 'grubstreet' means something of low literary value.*

In 2016, daily newspapers reached 757 million people worldwide, and generated $153billion in revenue.

The biggest circulation newspaper on the planet is the 9m-selling *Yomiuri Shimbun* in Japan, with 15 of the other top 20 all based in China, Japan or India. Three are American, one German, and the UK's widest read paper The Sun doesn't even feature, having a measly 1.5m readers.

According to the BBC's Global Audience Measure, in 2016 it reached 372m people globally every week. Technically that's twice the readership British newspapers can claim in print and online, but seeing as the Beeb mostly purloins its stories from newspapers, it should more accurately be recognised as a (unremunerated) form of guerilla marketing. More people rely on Fleet Street than at any point in human history. Point that out next time someone says they don't buy a newspaper any more, or asks why politicians still give a stuff what journalists write.

To their detractors journalists are known as 'hacks'. Although intended as an insult, it's rarely perceived as one. Churning out copy, at short notice and in return for payment, was thought low-class by those who considered themselves high-class. But many of our greatest literary giants paid the rent and honed their skills this way, and thousands of people still do the same.

If accused of hackery, quote Samuel Johnson on the same topic: *'No man but a blockhead ever wrote, except for money.'*

Point out that Daniel Defoe spent three days in a pillory in 1703 for writing seditious libel, and had flowers hurled at him rather than rotten vegetables. Or perhaps explain that

Charles Dickens started out as a Parliamentary reporter at a time when it was common to take your quotes to an MP for editing before they were published.

Any journalist stands a little straighter, and sticks their chin out a little further, if called a hack. Journalism involves short cuts, rough chops, unauthorised access, poor coping mechanisms and a nasty cough, and all may accurately be called a hack.

DO SAY: *'When Dickens was invited to become an MP he refused to return to Parliament on the grounds he could not stand to listen to another worthless speech.'*

DON'T SAY: *'So, Boris Johnson was fired from the Times for making up quotes from his own godfather. He'd make a great Prime Minister.'*

Fleet Street is the only road in the world that stretches from London to Accra and Sydney, by way of Jakarta, Beijing, Honolulu and almost every town and village in between. But the only part of the planet where newspaper circulation is rising is in Asia – everywhere else, print is in decline and people are instead reaching for the TV remote and internet.

The news cycle has gone from being the weeks it took to ride a horse, hear the news, compose the type, print the paper and outwit the Stationers' Men to being a 24-hour rolling digital knee-jerk of outrage, offence and dissembling.

There is little time for thought, but it was ever thus in Fleet Street. There is always something more exciting on the next page.

WHOPPERS FROM WAPPING

In 1986 the media baron Rupert Murdoch broke the first rule of journalism, which is 'never become the story'. Every newspaper was being held to ransom by militant print unions – sometimes even stopping production entirely over the simplest of disputes. It was inevitable newspaper owners would seize on new technology that would enable them to do without 90% of the 'inkies'.

But while most outlets went into negotiations and redundancy programmes, Murdoch's News International went to war. Executives swore there were no plans to de-unionise, then overnight moved staff from Grays Inn Road and Bouverie Street to a new complex in Wapping, and taught them how to send pages digitally straight to the press. Around 6,000 printers were sacked en masse, exploiting the Thatcher government's anti-union laws.

The National Union of Journalists (NUJ) ordered its members to strike, and most refused. Hacks were bussed into the plant through stone-throwing picket lines guarded by mounted and riot police. There were debates in Parliament, 400 policemen injured, 1,200 arrests, and one man killed by a delivery truck. At one point 20,000 people marched on Fortress Wapping, and it became a battlefield between Left and Right.

The strike collapsed after a year. Murdoch had, arguably, saved the newspaper industry. In his wake every newspaper moved out of Fleet Street to cheaper premises, digitised, modernised, and improved. The main union lost all its assets in the court battle, Murdoch earned Thatcher's lifelong approval and Labour's eternal loathing. The savings were used to set up Sky TV, expanding Murdoch's reach. Halfway through the dispute, when the NUJ held a ballot on strike action, hacks were persuaded to remain loyal with a pay rise and gym. The inkies never forgave them, and the NUJ seems to still bear a grudge too.

And Fleet Street became, and remains, more than just a place in London and a metonym for the British newspaper industry. For many, it's a way of life.

ß

'A man who exposes himself when he is intoxicated, has not the art of getting drunk'

Samuel Johnson

WHO'S WHO IN THE NEWSROOM

Walking into a newsroom for the first time is like walking into a riot. You're not sure who's fighting who, it's dirtier than you expected, and everybody seems to be under the influence of alcohol or narcotics, or both. There's only one way to survive – get your back against something solid, and keep your wits about you.

It used to be that newsrooms were filled with the sound of clattering typewriters, fistfights and crashing telephone receivers. These days they're more like the small claims department of a provincial insurance firm, filled with the sound of computer keyboards and weeping as the latest redundancy notices drop.

Phones still get thrown though, especially if work paid for them. Some things never change.

It may help to realise that newsrooms are run like an army (albeit a dysfunctional one) – a general at the top, infantry at the bottom, with junior officers in between, and everyone mutinous about something.

These units can be roughly broken down into news, features, pictures, sport, showbiz and online. Each department has its own desk, staffed by a minor editor, in charge of sending foot-soldiers out against the enemy (that's the rest of the human race; it will help to understand that journalists believe they're a different species, and that they may even be right).

These regiments battle to get stories published every day. Sometimes they co-operate, but more often than not the ground troops are gouging chunks out of each other as well as the target of their inquiries.

At the same time everyone on the field is regularly shelled by top brass who consider bullying to be vital to morale.

While newspapers, websites, TV and radio stations have slightly different ways of doing things, they all follow similar rules.

REPORTERS

The newsdesk fills the front of the paper, and top of the bulletins. The infantry are the reporters, easily identified by their worn-out shoes and weatherproof coats. They chase politicians through Westminster, sit on rainy doorsteps in mid-Wales, and fight through a press pack to get questions answered by a minor celebrity, often all in the same day.

A reporter will always have about their person a means of recording quotes, be it a notebook or digital device, and you can state with absolute authority that the only equipment that still works in the rain is a blunted pencil. They always have a driving licence, sometimes even in their own name. Aside from the shoes, reporters are usually smartly dressed as their working day could involve deathknocks (see page 126), covering a Royal visit or being photographed for a consumer-rights piece as a career conman kicks their head in.

The reporter's mantra is: "File by three, home for tea." They are the quickest journalists you'll ever meet.

BLUFFER'S TIP: *Many reporters start in local journalism, where a common task is to write up results of flower shows, school plays and gymkhana reports. Lists of names are a spelling minefield, but take special care of anything to do with horses – mothers of girls with a pony are terrifying if you get their little darling's name wrong.*

Older reporters will use only shorthand, which is illegible to anyone but themselves and can be said with confidence to definitely include the quote used in the paper ('it's that squiggle there, Your Honour'). Younger ones will use only a digital recorder, which proves conclusively no such quote was uttered ('oh dear, I should have learned shorthand').

Due to long periods spent 'on the road', reporters have bladders tougher than tungsten and are habituated to all forms of mental and physical abuse, both the giving and receiving of. They often include specialists, for example parliamentary, defence or royal reporters. They are the same as other reporters, but slightly lazier. By concentrating on one topic they have carved a niche for themselves, which they maintain with regular, but occasional, forays out of the office or onto the front page. The only thing which animates them is finding out a younger, fresher hack not only wants their job, but appears to be better at it. Don't poke this bear unless you really are.

NEWSDESKS

All reporters are 'run' by the newsdesk, which usually consists of a news editor, a deputy, and one or more assistant news editors. If you are lucky, one of them will have been a good reporter in a previous life and knows what a story looks like. More likely, they will have been such bad reporters that it was decided to keep them in the office out of harm's way. By promoting them to the desk, some idiot has given them power.

News editors have short fuses and respond to the unending pressure of their job with screaming, sweary meltdowns two or three times an hour. This usually happens while following 'the wires' - breaking stories fed in to the newsroom by agencies - or watching 24-hour rolling TV news, which will inform them that a lacklustre member of staff has just been scooped and is in need of a bollocking.

They thoroughly resent reporters for having more fun than they do. They know every trick a reporter has ever tried to skive off or cover their mistakes, so bluffers must tread carefully. If you annoy them you are likely to find yourself on a pre-dawn doorstep of a dog-fighting gang; if you impress them, you may find yourself in exactly the same place but with more expected of you.

News editors compile the stories reporters are working on into a 'news list' and present it in conference to The Editor, explaining the exclusive angle hacks have found while pretending they came up with it themselves.

Deal with them as you would a madman with a gun – a frank and non-confrontational manner, simple words and extreme caution.

BLUFFER'S TIP: *To bluff someone in news, pretend to be extremely drunk, then pull off the story of a lifetime just before deadline. Pour beer on your clothes, dip your hair in an ash tray, and rub soap in each eye to cultivate a bloodshot look before casually asking if your story about Meghan's secret lover is of interest.*

On a daily basis you will need to bluff the newsdesk into believing that a) it wasn't your fault and b) you're hard at work while having skived off hours ago. The canny bluffer rings the office to say the story's not working out, but you've got one more thing to try, and you're going to give it another couple of hours before you knock it on the head. Don't forget to say there's terrible reception, "what's that, hello?" and turn your phone off.

FEATURES DESKS

Features can be anything from interviews with a victim of crime to 1,000-word thoughtful analyses of the female orgasm, this season's must-have dress or the true story of Rorke's Drift. Its staff are considered by others to be soft-bellied desk johnnies who couldn't tell a story in 10 words if you held a gun to their heads.

Feature writers are mostly female, highly competitive, devastatingly caustic, and more than likely, when threatened, to use underhand tactics such as answering your phone and telling contacts that you've been fired, and to give all the stories to *them* from now on.

They are always on the latest diet, terrified someone else's diet is working better, and while being emotionally vulnerable to every little slight have the same searing focus on career progression as a laser cutting through lead. Feature writers fill the lifestyle sections in the middle of the paper, and pad out the last half of bulletins. They might specialise in fashion, arts, lifestyle or health. They have longer lead times than the news reporters, and prove the rule that the more time someone has to write, the worse their writing is. They have impressive contact books – while news reporters will throw anyone under the bus for a story, features tend to cultivate contacts. If you want to speak to an expert philatelist, a transgender physicist, or a convicted philanthropist, your best bet will always be asking a feature writer if they have one in their back pocket.

BLUFFER'S TIP: *The only way to impress a features writer is to let them know you are friends with The Editor, or sleeping with an all-powerful showbiz agent who can get them an interview with the biggest celebrity of the day. Be warned: they'll never leave you alone.*

Feature writers are less likely to meet real people, so dress with a certain amount of… originality. Some go for designer togs, others head-to-toe in junk shop chic.

Features editors have the power to create new columnists, commission articles, give or deny a freelancer a lucrative double-page spread, and cultivate the friendship of The Editor, occasionally with success. They have plenty of space to fill and more time to do it, which gives them the leisure to be kind or cruel depending on their whim. They all want to be The Editor next. Most of them will be.

Never underestimate people in features. They are highly-skilled at the assassin's art of interviewing, and can draw secrets out of you easier than rolling a tapeworm onto a stick.

COLUMNISTS

From among features' ranks columnists are sometimes plucked. You will know who in a newsroom is the columnist because they have the loudest voice in the building; it is a job designed for the sort of person who will climb on the bar to inform the pub's patrons why they're wrong about Brexit. Increasingly this coveted role is given to TV sorts and minor celebrities, but there are still a few old hands who got there by dint of having a lot of opinions.

SHOWBIZ

This desk breaks all the rules. It can be part of news or features, or allowed its own department. There will be junior staff who act as showbiz reporters doing the grunt work, showbiz writers a little further up the ladder who do interviews, and showbiz editors who steal the best stuff for their own byline. They're the same as all other journalists, but more likely to be cutting deals with agents in return for favourable coverage, and operating with an extreme hangover. They live on party nibbles and cheap champagne, and if they don't have drugs on their person they know who does.

PICTURE DESKS

Whether in newspapers or TV, the people who deliver the pictures are just as important as those who do the words. They are technically brilliant, socially appalling and scientifically fascinating. Picture editors are pretty much the same, but wash more regularly.

Phots, togs, toggies, snappers or whatever other name they are known by have a loathe-hate relationship with all words people. Hacks are despised for calling the office with a story they've just made up to cover their own backs, which gets the snapper in trouble for not having pictures of a thing that didn't happen. Alternatively, the snapper gets the pictures while the hack is buying the teas (on expenses) and has to pull their incompetent arse out of the fire.

DO SAY: *'Video-journalists are just trainees with a smartphone'*
DON'T SAY: *'Photo-journalist means anyone whose captions are more than 10 words long'*

Photographers call all writers 'blunts', which refers to the state of their pencils and is also rhyming slang for what they really think. In return, reporters and feature writers in all parts of the media call photographers 'monkeys', because they tend to gather in groups, hoot wordlessly, and wave their willies around.

BLUFFER'S TIP: *Never, ever, call a photographer a monkey in his or her hearing. It is deeply offensive, and as certain to earn their enmity as announcing you are teetotal.*

Always be nice to them. Without pictures, your story won't be published or broadcast, and they have a level of commitment which enables them to stare through a lens, unblinking, for days at a time to get the shot. There are few people who won't flinch in a riot or war zone, but everyone with a camera can adjust for focus and light while taking fire and at the same time let you know someone's coming up behind with a rock.

Furthermore, you will find that whoever your friends in the newsroom may be, it will be a photographer or cameraman next to you in the passenger seat, in the bushes, on the plane, in the ditch, or venturing into the dark heart of Doncaster. You will come to know and need them more than any other colleague, share more formative experiences, and rely on them for safety, comradeship and receipts. These blood brothers are a hack's best friend and most implacable enemy. Show them respect.

The bit about the willies is true, though.

CORRESPONDENTS

Officially, the most important, well-connected, and brilliant journalists in the newsroom. Unofficially, overpaid old farts who've been there 1,000 years, couldn't be fired, so got a title instead. Tends to swan about on foreign jaunts, steal bylines, and go for lunch with The Editor before filing screeds of impenetrable copy that is printed, inexplicably, word for dire word.

WEB EDITORS

Like news editors, but with 24-hour shift patterns and a smaller sense of fun. Also known as heads of content, because what goes on the web often isn't news. They chase clicks and page views, and unlike news editors know exactly whether anybody's reading the stuff their infantry pump out; never try to bluff them about how popular your work is, for they know the truth.

They are generally calmer, and a little more hard-working, than those in print or TV. They are distrusting of daylight and desperate to get a story on The Drudge Report. Show them kindness, file quickly, and don't hurt them. If you want to bluff your way onto the top of the homepage, all you have to do is find a way to get Kim Kardashian's arse in the headline.

Much the same can be said of online columnists, reporters, and feature writers, who have to not only get the stories, write the interviews and get it all right, but have to do it in such a way it gets clicks too. Bluffers will commiserate with them about the viral impact of the latest video by Dr Pimple Popper, while adding sagely that at least online staff know how to engage with the reader. They are terrified only of MailOnline, and impressed only by MailOnline.

SPORTS DESKS

A harmless, cliquey bunch with anorak-level knowledge of their chosen fields. A bluffer needs to know that sports reporters are what you'd expect, while sports *writers* are paid more to do less, but with more clout.

The sports department's analysis is always wildly off and the only thing they dislike is that period between summer athletics and the start of the football season. Sports editors are, usually, the only people in a newsroom with a vaguely happy home life. Bluff them with detailed knowledge of an arcane minority sport that is suddenly flavour-of-the-moment – Olympic curling, disabled lacrosse, or water polo. Never bet on their racing tips.

BLUFFER'S TIP:

The two most important things to remember when dealing with anyone in a newsroom are:

1) *Use the spellchecker*
2) *Newsroom people all start the day with a blank piece of paper, by lunchtime are prepared to die for a story, and by evening have forgotten it in a blur of alcohol. Throughout it all they are verbally, physically and mentally abused by almost everyone they meet or speak to. The next day, they get out of bed and do it all again, and they actually enjoy it.*

———————— *ß* ————————

'Reporters go through four stages in a war zone. In the first stage, you're Superman, invincible. In the second, you're aware that things are dangerous and you need to be careful. In the third, you conclude that math and probability are working against you. In the fourth, you know you're going to die because you've played the game too long. I was drifting into stage three.'

Richard Engel, American journalist and author

TOP BRASS

THE EDITOR

The Editor is a dictator, and knows it. Highly Machiavellian, they foster friendships with politicians and billionaires while undermining their own deputies, promoting staff purely to upset rivals, and destroying the mental stability of at least two random employees every day. They treat PAs like slaves, desk editors as scum, subs with extreme camaraderie (no-one gets to the top without the support of the subs), and their infantry as something they stepped in by accident.

Editors bear overall responsibility for whatever is published or broadcast, and are therefore best at blaming others. Editors can and have gone before the courts, and once or twice to jail, for things their staff have done, so they regard the entire newsroom with deep mistrust. The male of the species is generally scared of women; the female is just generally scary.

BLUFFER'S TIP: *Being called in to The Editor's office is like going to confession – you stare at the floor and hope they* *don't know what you did. Whether being bollocked or praised one thing is vital – TAKE YOUR NOTEBOOK. If The Editor is in two minds about whether to fire you, a notebook will make you seem halfway competent.*

It is their job to run conference, usually daily and sometimes twice a day, in which all desks present their lists. In some newsrooms this is a collaborative process, and in others it's ritual torture. Those present must be braced to answer any question, about any story, on their list or that otherwise pops into The Editor's head. It is possible to bluff your way through conference, but the price will be that once out of it you will have to deliver what you just promised.

The Editor's rages are universally feared. They can be loud, but the worst are quiet. The only way to get through them is to adopt the same position of abject apology as a Japanese car manufacturer caught fiddling emissions tests. Their obsessions can last weeks, and at some point every hack will be given an entirely bonkers 'editor's special' to work on, be it proving that petrol stations are run by an Icelandic Mafia, or that tins of Quality Street are not as chocolatey as they used to be.

Any attempt to bluff The Editor by claiming you are capable of greater things may mean you are asked to prove it. All Editors realise that they have a shorter top-flight career than a Premiership footballer with a limp, and spend every day defending their position in the hierarchy. Their chief flunkey is their only ally – a deputy editor, PA or someone with brackets in their title whose fundamental role is doing The Editor's dirty work while kissing their behind. If you want influence with

The Editor, it's the flunkey you must cultivate – there's nothing a slave likes more than a slave of their own.

THE EDITOR'S PA

This person wields the most power in any newsroom. They are the gatekeeper, aide-de-camp and eyewitness to The Editor, and are often treated appallingly by them. But never imagine that they will take your side in a face-off; their survival instincts are far too highly developed to do anything so rash. But use every opportunity to forge some sort of relationship with them. They're much too important to ignore.

Most desks have a secretary dedicated to doing their paperwork, and together with the editor's PA they form a gossip network that knows everything about everyone.

Occasionally these staff are the conscience of a newsroom – as the only non-journalists in the office, some editors have resorted to asking the nearest 'normal' person if this or that story seems unfair, before it is published. It's known as OFSEC.

BLUFFER'S TIP: *Never try to bluff a newsroom secretary. They know exactly what you're doing. Genuine sympathy for whatever menial task they've been given by their lunatic of a boss is the only way to win their hearts.*

MANAGING EDITORS

These people are former executives who've made a misstep and wound up in charge of the paper clips. It's their job to 'manage' the office. In theory it may involve running a graduate trainee scheme, overseeing budgets, liaising with personnel departments (increasingly known as 'HR' or, to their victims, 'Human Remains') and demanding computer upgrades. In reality it means avoiding trainees, telling desks there's no money, long lunches and ordering the stationery.

They are frustrated by no longer being at the sharp end of journalism, while delighted not to have died doing it. They are the ultimate arbiter of your expenses, and have the power to withhold part or all of a claim for spurious reasons.

BLUFFER'S TIP: *If asked to 'explain' your expenses, offer an explanation so outlandish that it becomes an anecdote for managing editors to delight their chums with. So while you may have claimed it was 104 miles from Peckham to Gatwick when it is nearer 30, you took an extreme detour in order to shake off a determined pursuit from Special Branch.*

EDITORS WITH BRACKETS IN THEIR TITLES

People who wanted to be editor, or used to be editor, and were given brackets to placate or demote them because they *Know Too Much*. Examples include Editor (Special Projects), Editor (Graduate Programme) and Editor (Investigations). They never produce any stories worth the name, but always look busy and are ridiculously well-paid.

PROPRIETORS

These used to be the news barons who owned newspapers, toppled governments and appeased fascism. Now they're more likely to be foreign fund managers, corporate chief executives, or bored billionaires. Some understand journalism, but most don't think it necessary.

They are focused on the bottom line, yet want to pretend they are 'newsmen', and interfere in whatever the journalists are doing to the detriment of all.

These people have the power to pull your story because it involves a major advertiser, and without the ethics to realise they shouldn't. They are the only ones left with big cars and drivers, and unlike The Editor can escape the consequences of cock-ups unless it negatively affects the share price.

BLUFFER'S TIP: *The only way to bluff a proprietor is to wriggle into the family's social circle. Help their spouse with a charity project, offer to keep a personal eye on a teenaged child during an internship, or if particularly brave try dating their daughter.*

If you can also manage to revise the closing share prices of the FTSE100, and discuss them knowledgeably with The Proprietor, you are guaranteed a job with brackets in the title.

'Journalism can never be silent: that is its greatest virtue and its greatest fault'.

Henry Anatole Grunwald

UNSUNG HEROES

SUB-EDITORS

These are the people whom it will most benefit you to befriend. They put copy on the page, trim it to fit the space and write headlines and picture captions, and depending on how they feel about you, they might turn 800 words of tear-jerking beauty into a 50-word NIB (see Glossary) on page 38. Or they can take your drunken downpage disaster and render it into prose suitable to grace the 4/5pp spread.

They weed out spelling errors, typos and poor grammar, and may entirely rewrite copy to better reflect The Editor's psychoses. They also act as unofficial alibi, in that any published error can be blamed on them rather than the reporter's own deficiencies. For example: "I put that quote in exactly as you said it, but the bloody sub changed it."

Subs have an encyclopaedic knowledge of literally everything. You can never bluff them, so instead show them you are their ignorant inferior and awe-struck at their greatness. Never disrespect a sub: this group are the most aggressively unionised, and most hardened drinkers in a newsroom. Insult one, and you insult them all.

SECTION EDITORS

These days many such titles should come with the initials RIP after their names, as City, Foreign, Travel, Health and other desks have been minimalised, merged, outsourced to freelancers or disbanded altogether.

Should you find one still clinging to their chair, however, they can be useful. City editors often have good stock market information, foreign editors can be mined for details of the best restaurants in Karachi, travel editors are beloved by all staff for handing out freebie foreign trips, and health editors have it within their gift to send you on a spa weekend.

Never take without giving from these last outriders of Fleet Street largesse. If you don't repay them with an inside tip, a story, or a jar of body scrub, they will never forgive.

LEADER WRITERS

A mate of The Editor given the job of writing no more than a few hundred words for the column that is theoretically the 'voice' of a newspaper and in reality an outlet for The Editor's crazed inner monologue. They have all bluffed their way into a high-pay, low-work position, and to do the same you will need to be the person best able to translate The Editor's ramblings into a mostly-coherent 250 words

FREELANCERS

These brave souls are lone wolves who fend for themselves in the wilds of self-employment, while getting paid increasingly less by desks and offering them stories they don't want to publish. Or they may form news agencies, covering a particular geographical patch or specialism such as the High Court or Parliament, with a crew of reporters doing distant doorknocks and fighting tooth-and-nail to get on the nationals.

LAWYERS

Lawyers delight in killing stories, as it proves their worth. They're also on speed-dial for hacks who run into trouble. Occasionally they may have background about a target's previous legal forays with the media to guide your hand *before* you libel them.

Their job is basically that of firefighter, except the fire keeps rewriting the rules about what can burn you. So they must keep updated with every new law, deal with threats from targets of inquiry, and respond to complaints from The Reader, politicians and the regulator.

If there is an issue with your journalism the lawyer will demand you produce a note, recording, or photograph, to back up your story. You can bluff them only as far as your evidence, and legal knowledge, can get you.

BLUFFER'S TIP: *Newsroom lawyers are more risk-averse than a hedgehog in a firework factory, and far spikier. But they all like to think they fight tooth and nail to get stories published. Make it clear you consider them in the vanguard of the Press freedom battle, with expertise that cannot be matched by any hack.*

STRINGERS

A final, and archaic, part of the journalistic mix. Once paid retainers but now mostly forgotten, this is a freelancer operating in a far-flung location whom the desk will instruct to get working on a story they cannot get to, for reasons of geography, war or expense.

BLUFFER'S TIP: *To boost your CV, try claiming to be a stringer. Send a few articles you've cobbled together to foreign papers or niche parts of the trade press. A good wheeze is to produce reviews and send them to arts magazines and Sunday supplements. Ask to be put on their books as a stringer. They'll never contact or pay you, but should anyone later check whether you really did have something published in the cinema section of the Vicksburg Gazette, they might find an old email and confirm you're one of theirs. Bingo, you're an internationally-recognised film critic!*

ASSORTED LOW LIFE

Page designers draw up the pages, usually in complete ignorance of which stories need to be fitted on them, while **artists** create logos, graphics, charts and other fiddly bits.

In every newsroom there are **trainees,** brought in on terrible pay to gain a qualification, and **interns** paid nothing to gain experience, which is more useful but does not cover the rent.

Occasionally people from **advertising** and **marketing** will appear, but they are usually more petrified of journalists than the other way around. Tell them that without them there'd be no news reported at all, and they'll look upon you with something close to devotion.

Finally, beware anyone from the **'Human Resources'** department, (formerly known as 'Personnel'). They are vainly seeking ways to carry out Top Brass's diktats to cut out dead wood (while mishandling any staff complaints). Never catch their eye.

'If Paris goes kablooey I want the best reporter I've got right there in the middle of it'

Perry White, *Superman II*

KNOW THINE ENEMY

Journalists like to think of themselves on the right side of history, fighting injustice with their bare, ink-stained hands.

Female columnists might talk about the campaigns of Jean Rook or the wit of Marina Hyde, reporters will grow misty-eyed talking of Bob Woodward and Carl Bernstein, and anyone who considers themselves an interviewer will be trying to channel David Frost when he had Richard Nixon on the ropes.

Journalists usually use the same methods for their entire career, with little variation in technique, and can therefore be put into one of six categories:

1. Muckrakers

Muckrakers are what you'd expect – the artfully shabby, persistent, Columbo-type bloodhound who digs into anything and anyone. While many look down their nose, it is these investigative journalists who work harder, for longer, and often put the authorities to shame with the evidence they find. Bluffers need to know that the greatest exponent of the art was also the father of modern tabloid journalism – a Victorian called W.T. Stead, who edited the Pall Mall Gazette and turned it from a gentleman's weekly into a thorn in the side of the Establishment. He introduced set-piece interviews, graphics and sub-headings and went into London's slums to write such lurid first-person accounts of the conditions that the government built better housing.

His greatest success was an investigation into child prostitution. Stead posed as a customer and 'purchased' 13-year-old Eliza Armstrong, daughter of a chimney sweep, to prove how easy it was.

He didn't operate with the best of ethics. Eliza, who was unaware of her role in the sting, was chloroformed, and later subjected to a virginity check before being returned to the family that had sold her. Stead was widely criticised for the stunt, which was also the first recorded instance of a journalist making the news, but public outrage meant Parliament passed a bill setting the age of consent at 16. Stead considered himself – as all journalists do - 'on the side of the angels'.

BLUFFER'S TIP: *Stead also produced the first 24-point headline, 'TOO LATE!' when the military failed to relieve General Gordon at the Siege of Khartoum in 1884. Even with his death he made news – Stead drowned on the Titanic in 1912, having given his life jacket to another passenger.*

2. It's All About Me

The natural progression of the star journalist is a hack who puts themselves in the story. The phrase 'gonzo journalism' was coined in 1970 to describe Hunter S. Thompson, an American author and journalist, who abandoned all pretence of objectivity and wrote in the first person, often while stoned. It's used as an insult by some, so bluffers need to know that 'gonzo' is Boston slang for the last man standing after an all-night bender, and whose recollections might be hazy and amusing but are all anyone has to go on.

Thompson died in 2005, leaving a legacy of peerless self-abusing, self destructive journalism. Bold moves are what typify this breed, who are most likely to bellow "look upon my deeds ye puny humans!". You always know when they're coming because their egos enter the room a good two minutes ahead of them.

These 'star' journalists are the ones who earn the big bucks, and grab the most readers, so belittle them at your peril. They're concerned only with their own brilliance, but feel free to bluff The Editor that you could do better given the chance, and cost considerably less.

3. What Idiot Believes This Stuff?

Anyone who has read Evelyn Waugh's *Scoop* may think his depiction of a war reporter who made up outlandish stories from the safety of their hotel room, forcing their competitors to race around to catch up, is fiction. In fact the type of journalists who make their competitors scream 'What Idiot Believes This Stuff?' are very much alive and well, and doing even better in the era of fake news. The most famous exponent is Boris Johnson who was made Brussels correspondent of the Daily Telegraph in 1989. Former colleagues on the same beat have since revealed he embellished stories so colourfully that people even today believe the EU banned bendy bananas, when it did no such thing. But that didn't stop editors lapping it up. Other correspondents were ordered by newsdesks to follow up these myths and find better examples, but as they didn't exist it was near impossible and he was bitterly resented. Boris himself said: "Everything I wrote from Brussels was having this amazing, explosive effect on the Tory party, and it really gave me this, I suppose, rather weird sense of power."

4. You're Great, You Are

The fourth category of journalist is perhaps the most successful in the world of television – the 'You're Great, You Are' school of sucking up to interviewees. A prime example is Michael Parkinson, whose chat show was favoured by celebrities because he didn't ask anything awkward, and got high ratings because he got the celebrities. He coaxed rather than confronted, laughed at their jokes, praised their talent, and sometimes got them to open up. The closest modern equivalent is Graham Norton, but his laugh is more annoying.

5. Come And Have A Go If You Think You're Hard Enough

The yin to Parky's yang is the Come And Have A Go If You Think You're Hard Enough types. These are the grand inquisitors who make Prime Ministers and chief executives quake. Examples are Jeremy Paxman, John Humphrys, and Nick Ferrari – pitbulls who maul an interviewee until they beg for mercy. Paxo asked Home

Secretary Michael Howard the same question 14 times when he refused to answer, while Ferrari has more recently put a severe dent in the reputation of Shadow Home Secretary Diane Abbott by catching her out on the maths of recruiting 10,000 police officers.

These confrontational journalists aim to trip people up, which is why they get good ratings. The print equivalent is Paul Dacre, editor of the Daily Mail who stepped down in 2018 after 26 years in charge of the most fearsome, powerful and irritating newspaper in Britain. A looming presence both in person and theory, he was the one editor whom every Prime Minister wished to charm, yet was most afraid of.

6. You Can Trust Me

Finally, and perhaps most famously, there are those journalists whose very appearance says Trust Me. In the USA, TV anchor Walter Cronkite was called the most trusted man in America, the reassuring voice of every historical moment from Kennedy's assassination to Nuremberg by way of the murder of John Lennon. The UK equivalent is David Dimbleby, who has anchored coverage of general elections, Royal weddings, state funerals, and major documentaries. He inherited the mantle from dad Richard, who was the first reporter to enter Belsen, and so treasured by audiences that 11 million people watched his funeral on TV. They are typified by the word 'gravitas' and there is a version in many newsrooms – the safe pair of hands to whom The Editor turns when disaster strikes, who can not only produce a decent story but render it the first draft of history.

It feels good to be this person, but you're not allowed to swear.

WHY EVERY HACK IS CLARK KENT

Journalists like to think of themselves in the mould of one of the greats, when actually there's only one sort of hack that everyone, male and female, wants to be: Lois Lane – dazzling, brilliant, The Editor's pet and love interest to a superhero, who also happens to be the world's biggest story and best source. In truth, all journalists are Clark Kent, bumbling through things they barely understand and often failing to get their underpants on properly. Which is why, no matter how successful they become, every journalist is bluffing furiously.

KNOWING THE BIG BEASTS

For effective bluffing, you will need to know that the biggest beasts in journalism are corporations. They include the **Daily Mail and General Trust,** which owns DMG Media, owner of the Daily Mail, Mail on Sunday, MailOnline, and Metro. The latter has now overtaken its sister paper the Daily Mail to become the country's most-read daily paper. DMGT sold its regional newspaper arm in 2012, but still reaches millions. It is owned by the last scion of the great newspaper barons: Jonathan Harmsworth, aka the 4th Viscount Rothermere. Its main competitor is **News UK**, which owns the Times, Sunday Times and Sun newspapers and websites and is controlled ultimately by billionaire Rupert Murdoch, aka The Great Satan. Perhaps the most prolific is **Reach plc,** which owns the Mirror, Express and Star titles, the People, Sunday Mail and Daily Record as well as hundreds of local newspapers and OK! magazine. It's ultimately controlled by shareholders, which is why it never has any cash. The **Guardian Media Group** owns the Guardian, Observer and guardian.co.uk, reaches 4.7m adults online every day but sells a paltry 135,000 copies a day (163,000 on Sundays) and lost £23m in the year to 2018. It keeps going because it has a £1bn endowment fund managed by a charity. Bringing up the rear are the **Telegraph Media Group** operated by Ritz-owning billionaire twins David and Frederick Barclay, and father and son Russian oligarchs **Alexander and Evgeny 'Two Beards' Lebedev,** who own the digital-only Independent and the Evening Standard. Baby sister the 'i' was sold in 2016 to Scottish newspaper group **Johnston Press (now JPI Media),** which with other regional giants **Local World** and **Newsquest** owns most of the local press in the UK.

Combined, they represent the mainstream print news brands in Britain and reach an audience in print, tablet, mobile and online formats, of 25m adults every day. Almost half of readers are aged 18-35, and in the year to April 2018 they notched up 920m interactions on social media compared to 880m for the BBC.

BLUFFER'S TIP: *TV types may crow that the BBC News At Ten is more popular than any UK newspaper, with 4.9m viewers. A bluffer will say that Strictly Come Dancing gets 13m and made Ed Balls seem fun, which proves the tabloid rule that you can't inform anyone if you don't entertain them first.*

DIGITAL FRIENDS

The brave new world of online journalism has seen hundreds of new start-ups, and a few are worth noting. Some aggregate news like the **Drudge Report**, picking the best and linking out to the original source; others like **BuzzFeed, Guido Fawkes** and the **Huffington Post** run their own journalistic teams with considerable success, while the likes of left-wing blogs such as **The Canary** and **Skwawkbox** have lots of readers but, at time of writing, can't spell 'objectivity' and have had too many feather-brained cock-ups to be taken seriously by most journalists, or indeed most chickens.

THE ENEMY WITHOUT

Once you've got your head around the enemy within, there is the enemy without. Showbiz agents and managers, official spokesmen and government minions, and press officers and public relations consultants who spend their days calling journalists and being ignored, begging them not to do something they therefore do twice as hard. But every journalist needs to know their principle enemy is also their best friend and driving purpose – **The Reader** (in the case of radio The Listener, and in TV, The Viewer). It is this one, imagined person they believe is paying attention that every journalist strives to satisfy, titillate and inform. If they are outraged, it must always be at someone else, for any journalist who upsets The Reader is not long for their job. Any news outlet that does so will face a collapse in share price. This is particularly difficult, because The Reader's moral compass spins more crazily than an ice skater on Monkey Dust. Which is why, throughout journalism, they're more darkly known as **The Bloody Reader.**

'When the going gets weird, the weird turn pro'

Hunter S. Thompson

NEW NEWS

People will tell you that the internet killed print journalism, but the bluffer knows better. Not many know it was the Royal Family that struck the first blow in 1953.

In that year the UK had a healthy national newspaper industry selling 15,790,000 copies every week – meaning approximately one third of the population bought one. By comparison, just 1% of homes had a TV set.

Newspapers could charge vast amounts for display adverts by big-name department stores. The classified sections alone could account for as much as 70% of a newspaper's income.

ROYAL BOX

Then Britain got a new young monarch, her consort Prince Philip was put in charge of the Coronation, and he decided to televise it. There was much upset among senior courtiers about losing "mystique". Newspapers worried about losing the scoop.

Prince Philip got his way, and everyone who could

afford it bought a TV. A total of 8 million people watched it at home, and another 10 million watched at a friend's. Newspaper sales peaked at the same time with souvenir editions, but it was short-lived.

Television ownership has grown in almost every year since, while newspapers had a near-constant downward trajectory. In 1981 Lady Diana Spencer married the Prince of Wales, and 28 million Brits watched on television. By 1983, academics were discussing whether the decline of newspaper readership was due to proprietors, tabloid practices or the unions, before reaching the conclusion that *"all these factors are only waves superimposed on an outgoing tide"*.*

Advertisers fled from print. Newspapers had to do something the TV news wasn't doing – so there was more showbiz, sleaze and naked opinion.

PAP SNAP

The public loved Diana and as her marriage broke down, big money was paid for images of the most photographed woman in the world. But it was TV the Royals turned to when they wanted to speak to the nation. Prince Philip (him again) did it first in 1961, and Charles got 14 million to watch his confession of adultery in 1994. Diana walloped him with 23 million viewers a year later for her 'princess of hearts' Panorama interview.

When she was killed in a Paris car crash in 1997,

* Robert L. Bishop, "The Decline of National Newspapers in the UK", *International Communication Gazette*, June 1983.

immense public rage was directed at the paparazzi who were pursuing her and the newspapers which paid them (not at the readers whose thirst contributed to the feeding frenzy). All editors promptly promised to ban 'pap' photos, then directed the public fury towards the Queen for not displaying grief. By the time of the funeral it was the Royals that The Reader loathed.

In the years that followed, the Press had to find a way of covering the Royal Family while honouring a pledge to leave Diana's sons alone. So Prince Edward was exposed when his own TV company flouted the agreement with a documentary into the princes, his wife Sophie and sister-in-law Sarah Ferguson were targeted by the News of the World's 'fake sheikh', and gradually pap photos of the rich and famous returned.

NET GROWTH

When the internet appeared in 1982 it had been barely noticed. When email arrived in 1993 it was just a quicker way of bollocking all the staff at once. A few newspapers launched rudimentary free-to-access websites, with the Guardian leading the way in 1999 and MailOnline following in 2003. When Facebook arrived in 2004, with Twitter on its coat tails two years later, the executives shrugged.

Two things changed newsroom attitudes. The first was the seventh series of Big Brother in 2006, which (if anyone cares) involved a punk with Tourette's, an anorexic version of the Tasmanian devil, and an ex-girlfriend of Mike Tyson.

In those days Big Brother was a national event, and whole newsrooms were devoted to uncovering backgrounds of housemates.

Previously, it involved knocking on doors, asking people questions and spamming a classful of people on Friends Reunited.

But by 2006 everything a journalist needed was on Facebook, where housemates had naively allowed public access to their friends, photographs and talkative ex-lovers. Overnight half of Fleet Street joined the site.

A year later, terrorists drove a Jeep loaded with propane through the front doors of Glasgow Airport. A security cordon was thrown up around the airport and none of the journalists who raced to the scene could get to the story.

Then someone had the bright idea of looking online. Social media was filled with images and quotes direct from people still trapped in the terminal building. People had even uploaded videos of the burning car that could be used on the evening news.

Baggage handler John Smeaton became a hero for kicking a terrorist in the testicles while shouting "f***in' c'mon, then!" He was later given the Queen's Gallantry Medal, which arguably would not have happened if those who'd witnessed him doing so hadn't recorded it.

The internet had come into its own, and finally the people in charge of newspapers realised its power. Websites were redesigned and upgraded, business plans re-examined, social media operatives employed. But it was not enough. Combined with the influence of rolling news TV stations like the BBC's News 24 launched in

1997 and Sky News in 1999, the internet's constant updates meant The Reader always had a fresher source of news.

PRESS PARADOX

The obvious choice was to invest in things the internet couldn't – investigations, analysis, campaigns.

Instead, the drive to get more stories for less money meant a greater focus on showbiz and famous love lives. Sex had sold since time immemorial, but now it paid the bills.

Computers, email and mobile phones were used to fake identities, track celebrity cars, and hack voicemails, with the resulting paradox that news was both more accurate and more illegal than it had been at any time since the Stationers' Men stalked Fleet Street.

And it was the Royal Family once again which gave a bloody nose to the Press.

Clive Goodman was Royal reporter for the News of the World, and made his name with stories about Diana. After her death his stock dropped, and editor Andy Coulson sidelined him by appointing a younger reporter to cover the same beat.

Subsequent court hearings revealed that Goodman contacted private investigator Glenn Mulcaire, and the two began hacking the voicemails of Royal staff. Prince William smelt a rat in 2005 when he started to read about things that had been mentioned only to a trusted few. His private secretary noticed that new voicemails were showing as having been listened to, and police were informed. The subsequent investigation found several phones in the Royal circle had been accessed by Goodman and Mulcaire, and the pair were sentenced to 4 months and 6 months respectively. (See page 107 for further background on hacking.)

BLUFFER'S TIP: *When discussing this with a journalist, express bemusement about hacks being jailed for hacking, and point out the stories they uncovered were not only true but lapped up enthusiastically by readers. When discussing it with The Reader, express disgust but point out that, had Jimmy Savile owned a mobile, he'd have been caught BEFORE he died.*

THE BIG CHILL

The scandal spread to other newspapers and had "a chilling effect"* on all journalists, in all media, whether involved or not.

Corporate legal bills mounted, the redundancy axe was re-sharpened and not only millions of pounds but centuries of experience went down the Fleet Street sewer.

Older hands took the pay-offs and ran. Younger, cheaper staff were hired to watch Instagram all day. Photographers went from being people who knew the law to being anyone with a smartphone.

As of January 2018, every national daily and Sunday newspaper was in decline except the Financial Times, which had a measly 0.35% increase in readership. But

---

* The words used by politicians and newspaper editors when stating that new statutory controls on the press would threaten democracy.

the national print titles are still courted by politicians, set the agenda, and are the main route by which scandals are exposed and investigated.

News has changed from being something we used to seek out and read thoughtfully, to a thing we are bombarded with 24 hours a day in a Twitterstorm of claim and counter-claim. Even when asleep we're notified via our smartphones of breaking news all over the world, which means as a species we are better connected, and have worse insomnia, than ever.

WHAT GOES AROUND...

TVs are now in 96% of all homes, but their viewing figures have been eaten into by other providers. In 2017 it was reported the average adult was watching 12% less TV than in 2010, and teenagers were watching a third less. In 2018, Ofcom revealed that streaming services like Netflix had overtaken the pay-TV giants, with 15.4 million customers.

BLUFFER'S TIP: *A job in print was once a necessary stepping stone to a more lucrative one in TV. Today you're better off building a social media following – if you can bring the audience, editors in any medium will fight over you.*

Newspapers have historically shown a cycle of boom and bust, and each time they survived by innovating around social change.

When the newspapers that began in the Civil War were refused licenses, the journalists simply published them abroad or in secret. When photography was invented and theoretically rendered an eyewitness useless, newspapers proved using both was better. And when computers came along, when colour printing was introduced, newspapers made the most of it. None of these things happened quickly, without scandal, or entirely to The Reader's satisfaction, but they happened. And the Royal Family has been at war with, and courted, the Press every step of the way.

Bluffers can counter the 'newspapers are finished' argument by pointing out that in 1947 the UK had 12 national newspapers that reached a third of the population. Today, it has 20 national newspapers whose combined reach in all formats is 37% of the country, and they have worldwide audiences too.

Their websites seek one thing above all else: video, which gets twice the engagement with readers. A print dinosaur who can evolve to break stories online in video format might just save us all – and if a video-journalist gets a Royal misbehaving on camera, it'd be even sweeter.

BLUFF YOUR WAY IN

The oft-quoted 'expenses culture' and lure of foreign travel, exotic interviewees and khaki-clad danger are enough to convince anyone they want to be a journalist. It used to be that if you hung around the wrong sort of pubs you'd bump into journalists eventually and could just ask for a job, but that's not something that could be described as a plan. Or indeed healthy.

THE FRONT DOOR

But there are several easy ways for any idiot to bluff their way into journalism through the front door:

1. Be the child of a journalist

All other journalists will instantly admire/fear/loathe you, and depending on the abilities of your parent you will find all doors are opened – if your parent's an idiot, of course, it will be a fire exit lined with knives. That's the risk you take

2. Be the child of someone more important than a journalist

Related to the chief constable? An MP? How about the ad director, The Editor's manicurist, a vice-admiral, or some other high-and-mighty? Perhaps you've been to a good school with the right sort of people. If you can present yourself as an excellent source of stories from family friends in high places, the red carpet will be rolled out for you.

3. Get a journalism degree

This might cost you north of £30,000 and three years of your life, but it's quicker and cheaper than Eton. Students will complain, because students always do, but those three years will involve the most helpful editors, the longest deadlines, and the fewest problems of any journalism you will ever perpetrate. Some courses are better than others, but to a student they all seem like hell; to a working journalist, a degree seems like a nice long rest without screaming.

You will find that while these get your foot in the door of most newsrooms, stopping yourself being thrown out again will require development of monumental bluffing skills.

Boris Johnson is the only known exception to this rule, and that's because despite his terrible writing, questionable fact-checking and regular public apologies, he is a headline generator. It is unlikely to work for bluffers, for what in Boris is considered charming would be a legal liability in others.

THE BACK DOOR

For the uninvited, there are other methods of gatecrashing the ink party:

1. Work experience

Also known as 'working for free', internships, school and student newspapers, and 'we can't afford proper staff' on certain websites. A means to gain experience, contacts and a bulging cuttings file. It provides a chance to schmooze, cajole, charm or harangue other journalists and to be an immediate replacement when someone flounces out or is fired.

Taking this route – working hard for a lucky break – will give you the skills needed to go far, which is why it's so successful. Three years on a local paper is always more useful than university, although increasingly those doing it are also expected to get a degree. There is no logical reason for this.

2a) Vocational qualification

These can add polish to a wannabe hack, for significantly less time and money. It's possible to get them straight after A-levels, or later in life for a career change. The gold standard is run by the National Council for the Training of Journalists, and you will find many older hacks growing tearful when discussing their NCTJ. Other options are available, including NVQs, BTECs and diplomas. They can last anything from 6 weeks to a year. Pick one that concentrates on shorthand, law, and actual publication and you won't go far wrong.

BLUFFER'S TIP: *The NCTJ journalism exams featured stories from the fictional settlement of Oxdown, a town twinned with disaster. It witnessed air crashes, rail smashes, drug epidemics and killing sprees, and every resident and road had an oddly-spelled name. Tell people you wish you'd worked there, but never put 'Oxdown Gazette' on the CV.*

2b) Indentured training

This is rarer than it was, but still available to those who represent a reasonable investment for The Editor's shrinking budget. Mostly to be found in local media, but with a few highly-prized graduate programmes with national outlets, it combines a fixed-term contract with training, giving the lucky few both a wage and a qualification. The Editor too gets the cheapest hacks they will ever employ, and the comforting belief they are keeping the flame of Fleet Street alive.

BLUFFER'S TIP: *Abandoning this particular slave ship will earn you the undying enmity of The Editor, and should you ever cross their path again you won't just be toast, but sliced, diced and turned into cat food.*

3. Blogging

Every aspiring journalist has a blog, and they are mostly self-centred, badly-spelled and barely-read. This is a public CV and the first thing any future employer with the most basic of internet skills will see. It is also a means of demonstrating that you can personally bring in new readers, which is all anybody wants.

So ensure it has content covering your intended

field. Don't apply for sports jobs yet have a blog that does music reviews. Market with social media, work to get it widely-read, and mention the unique visitor numbers in job applications. Only the blog author can see these so you have some leeway with the truth, but don't go sticking six zeroes on the end unless you really are the new Perez Hilton. Under this heading could also be lumped podcasts, YouTube channels and anything else that might be useful in the brave new world of online journalism.

BLUFFER'S TIP: *Don't put anything online under your own name that you don't want future colleagues or editors to see. If you really must blog about your sex life, use a fake name, and if there are any racy pictures make sure your face isn't in them, for a degree of plausible denial.*

And for the truly desperate:

4. Trade press

In-flight mags, corporate publications, or even those dire Pravda-style compilations of local authorities will give you a (small) wage while publishing your words. The downside is that there are few journalists to impress, and no Reader to speak of.

But it can be career-defining. The highly-specialised Inside Housing was the only publication to report on the fire fears of residents in high-rise tower blocks, and was proven horribly right with the Grenfell Tower blaze that killed 72 people. Specialist publications on railways and the health service often sniff out scandals.

You might find yourself on the right sort of magazine when that industry is suddenly at the centre of a huge story, and have the contacts to land a specialist job on the nationals.

You might also find yourself rewriting Pippa Middleton's drivel for Waitrose magazine for the rest of your life. Which is why you need to be desperate.

FOOT IN THE DOOR

There are many ways in, but do not dismiss those journalists who had an easy road into the trade. If they have survived more than a month in the job they will need to have proved they are worthy to work alongside the finest bluffers. They will also probably have read this book.

Getting your foot in the door is just the first, terrifying step. Regardless of how they get there, once in the business all journalists must prove they have the most important qualification of all – a level of enthusiasm that borders on mental illness.

M'LEARNED FRIENDS

Every journalist starts out thinking they will speak truth unto power. In fact, the only truth you will ever tell is the one you're allowed to.

Once you get over the multiple hurdles of space, time, budget constraints, what The Reader is interested in and what The Editor will allow, however much truth you are left with is passed through The Lawyer. By the time his red pen has done its work, your 8,000-word expose of government corruption could look more like a Department of Trade press release.

LAW AND ASSES

Britain is one of a handful of countries with an unwritten constitution, which means you're allowed to do anything unless it's banned, and the law is forever banning something new. Most nations prefer to write down what you can do, and call these things 'rights', whereas in the UK all citizens can do whatever isn't written down yet, but could carry a 10-year sentence next week.

Aspiring journalists may find it daunting, and feel the only laws which will apply are about defamation and alcohol licensing. Journalists who have been in the job for a week or so will know that just about every law in Britain can, has and will be used against them. Bluffers will affect an attitude of nonchalance towards the law, and will state authoritatively that the best example of it being an ass is a British police investigation into payments to police officers and other public officials which began in 2011.

OPERATION ELVEDEN

Conducted by the Metropolitan Police, Elveden was borne out of paperwork provided by executives at Rupert Murdoch's News International while it was under investigation for phone hacking. An internal trawl uncovered evidence of payments to public officials, and it is widely believed the documents were thrown up as chaff to divert police attention from hacking.

It was proof of multiple payments to soldiers, prison officers, coppers and their partners in return for stories. To an outraged public this was more evidence of journalistic foulness; to detectives rifling through Fleet Street's bins it was heinous corruption; to journalists, it was like being arrested for sharpening a pencil. We can't *write* otherwise, officer.

It spread, via 200,000 emails, bank accounts and career moves of journalists, to other newspapers. Police arrested 90 people, but there was no modern law to prosecute them with. Bluffers will note that chequebook journalism is not actually illegal.

In the absence of a single statute, the Crown Prosecution Service searched the legal vaults and blew the dust off an 800-year-old scroll which said all concerned could be charged with something called 'misconduct in public office' (MIPO).

This ancient bit of common law, based on precedent rather than an Act of Parliament, carried a maximum sentence of life imprisonment (a laughable punishment for bunging a contact £50 for a tip-off that never made the paper, but that's the law for you: a bit of a bugger for journalists).

It gets even more ass-like. Unfortunately for the CPS, journalists aren't public office holders, so could be prosecuted only for conspiring to commit the offence with someone who was. Conspiracy requires evidence of a firm agreement between two or more parties to commit a crime, and as hacks rarely write promises down in case they're ever held to them, every single reporter but one of the 34 arrested was cleared.

Their sources, however, were not. Nine police officers and 21 others were convicted, including a DCI who rang the NOTW to expose funds being diverted from counter-terrorism, but did no story with them; a prison officer who revealed child killer Jon Venables' comfy life in jail; and a policeman who told a hack that Zara Philips' handbag had been stolen.

In effect, a 13th century law terrified journalists and ruined careers of not only public interest whistleblowers but also harmless gossips.

No journalist had ever worried about that law

before, but they do now – mainly because Elveden did what the authorities wanted, and stopped public servants telling what they knew. Thus the law, without a single word being changed, made it impossible to tell a truth unless the source doesn't care about jail or their job.

HOW THE LAW WORKS

Journalists have no more legal rights than other citizens, but they tend to get the impression they have fewer.

Everyone is able to knock on someone's door and ask them a question, but a journalist who does so will be accused of trespass. Any fool can write they disapprove of burqas on social media, but do it in a newspaper and it becomes a hate crime.

You may need several approaches to the object of a story before they agree to talk to you, and be unfailingly polite each time. But under the 1997 Harassment Act if they've asked you once to go away then a second approach is enough to be arrested for stalking.

Laws are rarely brought in specifically with the intention of limiting journalism; they tend to do it accidentally. A prime example is the Bribery Act of 2010, which was aimed at ending big business corruption yet may also stop a journalist paying a barman for CCTV footage that proves a story.

Between 2011 and 2015 there were just 16 prosecutions under this law, most of them for things like someone attempting to persuade a driving examiner to issue a 'pass' after a failed driving test.

YUMAN RITES

But perhaps the law most commonly used to bully journalists is the privacy law that doesn't exist. There is no Privacy Act, no statute, no legislation which guarantees non-molestation by journalists because of 'privacy'.

There is only Article 8 of the Human Rights Act 1998, which is 17 words long. It states: "Everyone has the right to respect for his private and family life, his home and his correspondence." A good bluffer must be able to quote this confidently in a job or police interview.

BLUFFER'S TIP: *Arch a cynical eyebrow, and add that Article 8 allows for public authorities to interfere with this "right to respect" in the interests of detecting crime, protecting national security, upholding public morals, or defending the rights of others. All of these are vague enough that a local council is still somehow allowed to spy on people for putting their bins out on the wrong day.*

Journalists are regularly sued under the Act for breaching privacy by reporting on something someone would prefer they didn't but most people would rather they did.

Article 8 is in constant battle with Article 1, which allows for freedom of expression and opinion, as well as imparting information and ideas without interference. The courts regularly put one above the other, then change their minds. For example, in 2002 the extra-marital affair of former Manchester City footballer Garry Flitcroft led to a High Court privacy injunction that was broken by three newspapers. They won on appeal, with judges ruling the original court order was an "unjustified interference with the freedom of the press".

But in 2004 supermodel Naomi Campbell won a similar battle with the Daily Mirror, which had published photographs of her leaving a Narcotics Anonymous meeting. A first court hearing decided it was intrusive but awarded her a paltry £3,500 in damages, while a second declared it "a legitimate, if not essential, part of the journalistic package designed to demonstrate that Ms Campbell had been deceiving the public when she said she did not take drugs" and ordered that she pay £750,000 costs. A third ruled her "confidence was breached" and that SHE should be the one to get the costs paid to her.

Journalists can be forgiven for being confused.

BLUFFER'S TIP: *The final judgement ruled that revealing Ms Campbell was in NA was fine. It found against the Mirror because its story included details of her therapy, and the court felt it could deter her and others from seeking help. What you can and can't report is a fine line which is often invisible until after you've published.*

JUDICIAL ORDERS

All of this leads neatly into the world of **injunctions** and **superinjunctions**, and the sort of information that's definitely private yet just as definitely a justifiable story. These court orders are granted by civil courts to protect someone's privacy. Injunctions prevent publication, but the fact that the injunction exists can be reported. Superinjunctions ban anyone mentioning there was an injunction.

The superinjunction scandal came to a head in May 2011. A growing number of rumours about celebrities who'd paid to keep their scandals out of the papers turned into a spreadsheet, compiled by multiple authors with inside knowledge, and circulated widely on social media. It listed each injunction – anonymised by the courts with random letters from the alphabet, such as ABC vs XYZ – alongside the wrongdoer's real name and reported transgression.

The fact that thousands could see what their clients wanted hidden meant London's libel firms had a proper headache, with too many people to sue, and clients who started asking what, exactly, they were paying for.

By the end of the month growing numbers had named squeaky-clean Manchester United footballer Ryan Giggs, who had an injunction about an affair with former Big Brother housemate Imogen Thomas. His lawyers accused her of blackmailing him before she sold a kiss-and-tell about an anonymous footballer, and the Sun was stopped from identifying him.

After 75,000 people named Giggs online, and Scottish newspapers not bound by English law stuck him on the front pages, MP John Hemming named him in Parliament, which allowed English newspapers to report it and made the injunction useless.

Superinjunctions had sparked the biggest incidence of mass civil disobedience since the Peasants' Revolt of 1381, and proved judges couldn't block the information superhighway. For Giggs it led to further revelations about a long fling with his sister-in-law, and the eventual end of his marriage. He also had to admit Thomas wasn't a blackmailer, which made the whole thing an expensive waste of time.

BLUFFER'S TIP: *In these circumstances always mention the cautionary 'Streisand Effect' – namely, drawing attention to something you wish to keep private, and thereby publicising it. The Giggs Effect is the result of claiming secrecy because you're innocent, thus alerting journalists to the possibility of your guilt.*

RIPA WHAT YOU SOW

Before the phone-hacking scandal, trainee hacks were not informed that intercepting telecommunications was illegal (although it has been since the **Regulation of Investigatory Powers Act 2000,** which has no public interest defence), with those consequently in the dock regularly claiming they believed it an immoral shortcut rather than a crime. Courts are increasingly willing to make judgements in libel and privacy cases against the likes of Google and Facebook, although they're mostly unenforceable, and under the same RIPA law anyone can be prosecuted for not giving up social media, computer and phone passwords.

Journalists have no immunity, and might not even know when their communications are scrutinised. In 2012 Tory chief whip Andrew Mitchell was accused of swearing at police officers and calling them "plebs" while leaving Downing Street. The hunt for the mole involved detectives seizing the phone records of three Sun journalists to find the copper who leaked the story.

It led to Mitchell's resignation and eventual humiliation in a libel case; four officers being sacked and three disciplined; and another officer who pretended to be an eyewitness was given a 12-month sentence using our old friend MIPO.

The Sun took the issue to an information tribunal, which found the police were within the law with regard to two journalists but not the third, breached all of their rights to a respect for privacy, and found RIPA "did not adequately safeguard the important public interest in the right of a journalist to protect the identity of a source".

The government promised to amend the law to give journalists a defence, but it has since been revealed RIPA was used to access journalists' phone records on the Mail on Sunday, Daily Mirror, Northern Echo, Press Association and Sunday Mail, all of whom were investigating... the police!

MUTABLE LAWS

The main problem – and saving grace, depending whose side you're on – of an unwritten constitution is that the law can change with each new case, and change back again with the next. The period between the two is exploited by lawyers.

When Sir Cliff Richard took the BBC to court for hovering a helicopter over his house while announcing police were investigating historical sex allegations, the judge ruled his privacy was wrongly invaded by "sensationalist" coverage. The media feared it would make them unable to name suspects before they were charged, despite the judge's assurances to the contrary. And they rightly said sensationalism was legal.

Editors were perhaps thinking of the case of Rolf Harris, whose investigation was well-known but went unreported by Fleet Street for weeks after his lawyers wrote to newspapers claiming any coverage could seriously harm an old man's health. In the wake of Cliff's result, it happened again – several newspapers had letters quoting the judgement and claiming it applied to stories about other clients.

Sometimes it works to scare journalists this way, especially if the tale is one they're not that bothered about. But try it with a story big enough and it will become a hill they are prepared to die on. There will inevitably be a story which takes everyone back to court for a judgement in the opposite direction, after which journalists will feel emboldened until they overstep the mark and a court finds against them once more.

In an unwritten constitution, the law – and everything else to do with journalism – tends to be cyclical. The trick is knowing when you're on the upswing.

BLUFFER'S TIP: *Official secrets remain a sensitive area, and bluffers must be wary. In 1983 government clerk Sarah Tisdall anonymously sent photocopied documents about the imminent arrival of US Cruise missiles to the Guardian. Editor Peter Preston, who had no idea of her identity, fought a court battle to protect the papers but lost and was forced to hand them over. The authorities used them to find the photocopier, and Tisdall was jailed for four months. Preston never forgave himself for not destroying the papers.*

STRICTLY CLASSIFIED

The final bit of law bluffers should look out for and profess some familiarity with is the legendary D-notice:

an official request from government not to publish sensitive information about security matters, including military, intelligence and counter-terrorism techniques, plans and assets, or the nuclear deterrent.

If you get one, you must punch the air with delight and run yodeling three times around the newsroom, for it proves that not only is your story accurate, it's about a state secret and you've just scared the government witless. It's herogram time! D-notices (now known as DSMA notices*) are not legally binding, although many editors obey them. Depending on circumstances, a call from the D-Notice committee politely asking not to report something may be all it takes to get the yarn onto the front page.

PUSHING BACK

Amid all this legislative and ethical confusion, you must bear in mind that every journalist needs to watch their back.

If you do the crime, you'll serve the time, unless you can be confident of persuading a jury to acquit. For this high-risk bluff, the best rule of thumb is to rely on the advice of former Sunday Times editor Harold Evans, who said that journalists should never do anything to get a story that they wouldn't put in their copy. Above all things, remember it's a journalist's duty to push back against the law wherever possible, and especially where it isn't.

Reporting only what the authorities let you report isn't journalism. It's dictation.

* Defence and Security Media Advisory Notice

ß

'If I know Lois Lane, she'll not only come back with a Pulitzer Prize story, but a one-on-one interview with the hydrogen bomb titled What Makes Me Tick.'

Perry White, Superman II

PLAYING THE GAME

In days of yore cub reporters had to prove their worth in drinking contests with older staff. They were accepted into Fleet Street if they could show, not only that they would remain standing when others had fallen, but were still able to file copy afterwards.

When the Editor called morning conference, hacks hungover from the night before would shiver their way to the nearest pub for a heart-starter and a couple of pints, have a morning snooze in a courtroom press bench, then engage in a liquid lunch before filing some copy and retiring to the pub again about 3pm for a proper drink. After the paper was 'off-stone' (see Glossary) they would celebrate their exclusives or drown their sorrows until the pubs closed. They staggered into the newsroom next morning, facing the tyranny of a once-more empty paper, and needed a drink to deal with it.

If that reads like alcoholism to you, you'd be right. Journalists, however, take pride in being *functioning* alcoholics, which is much more skilled.

To a hack it is a badge of honour to have pulled off a great scoop while inebriated. The expert levels of bluffing involved meant drunks in Fleet Street were lionised, and great journalism became associated with industrial quantities of booze. There are still older subs who insist it is impossible to write a decent headline without a drink to loosen up, and plenty more who will claim the 'great writing while slumped over a bar' myth was perpetuated by people still in the pub, while the sub was rewriting their drivel.

All journalists, even in the glory days, would have been fired if they were *incapably* drunk at work. And even more so today, when heavy drinking is less socially acceptable.

But if called upon to journalise:

a) when drunk, try white bread and a glass of milk to sober up

b) when hungover, have a bacon sandwich and a large cup of sweet tea

c) when so hungover you're still drunk, only a Bloody Mary will do

LEGENDARY WATERING HOLES

The heroes of Fleet Street are often those who, in any other walk of life, would be in a secure hospital. So Jeffrey Bernard, who was too "unwell" to notice deadlines so often that a play was written about it, would ignore his editor from a bar stool at the **Coach & Horses** in Greek Street, Soho. All bluffers of a certain vintage must be able to recount a few lost afternoons with 'Jeff' (not forgetting that he died in 1997).

The French House in nearby Dean Street was patronised by heavy-drinking writers like Brendan Behan and Dylan Thomas, and so seemed both tolerant and glamorous enough for hacks to visit, and it might also be a source of stories.

Other drinking holes became famous, and commonly-used, because of where they were or who could be found in them.

Those who win a case at the High Court walk out the front door and over the road into **The George,** where journalists can find the successful litigant, buy them a bottle of champagne, and get the first chat. Those who lose may leave via the back entrance, opposite which is the smaller and more atmospheric **Seven Stars.** Any lawyers or defendants who wish to drown their sorrows will find a consolation pint, and by sheer coincidence a sympathetic journalist keen to report their tale of injustice.

BLUFFER'S TIP: *When at an awards ceremony, fill your boots on free booze only AFTER you've won or lost the gong. If you win, tell everyone it is a sign of the hard-won approval of your peers. If you lose, insist awards are a load of bollocks anyway.*

In Whitehall there lies the **Westminster Arms,** a favourite of politicians scheming between votes as it's within an easy canter of the division bell, and the **Red Lion** which is favoured by, well, the reds.

Many return to Fleet Street itself – the labyrinthine **Ye Olde Cheshire Cheese,** the stained-glass **Old Bell** next to St Bride's Church, and **El Vino's** wine bar which once refused to admit women, and then women in trousers, for years until the 20th century caught up with it. There's also the **Punch Tavern** which was so named in 1841 because the writers of Punch magazine spent so much time there.

Every newspaper would have a pub which its staff regarded as their territory. Journalists from papers other than the Daily Mail would wander into the **Mucky Duck** at their own risk; only Mirror staff were welcomed at the White Hart, more fondly known to its patrons and to history as **The Stab In The Back.**

Landlords quickly saw financial benefit in catering for hacks – they needed telephones, spare pens, painkillers and excuses. Newsdesks would frequently ring around the watering holes seeking AWOL staff. At the Stab there was a sliding scale of charges for barmen to say 'I haven't seen him' to whoever was asking – £1 for the newsdesk and £2 for wives. It is unknown what they charged for criminal kingpins looking to settle a score, but it probably involved an auction.

BLUFFER'S TIP: *Alcohol is a cheap truth drug because it makes it hard to lie without giggling. Try to remain more sober than your interviewee – ensure they eat nothing, but line your own stomach with a jacket potato and cheese.*

So it is that Private Eye calls its fictional reporter Lunchtime O'Booze, but most of these legends have long since shuffled off to the great saloon bar in the sky. Today, with the unceasing deadlines of the internet and pressure on budgets, journalists are more likely to be chained to their desks and barely allowed a damp sandwich at lunchtime. They might aspire to fruit smoothies and gym membership these days, but a good bluffer needs to remember two things:

1) They might not be alcoholics, but they're no healthier
2) They all still wish they were Jeffrey Bernard, and are secretly impressed with anyone who appears to be

BLUFFER'S TIP: *Only one legendary drunken hack trumps Jeffrey Bernard. You will, of course, have spent a lost weekend in the* **Woody Creek Tavern***, near Aspen, Colorado, drinking Chivas Regal with Hunter S Thompson before going out and shooting something. When asked what, shake your head ruefully and say you can't remember.*

For all the japes, there's a good reason journalists drink. News editors bully them, The Editor belittles them, colleagues indoctrinate them, and on top of that they see and hear absolute horrors – interview serial killers, dip in and out of wars, stand in aid tents surrounded by starving

Ways to sleep off a hangover without anyone noticing:
1. Get sent on a long, quiet doorstep
2. Locate the newsroom's disabled toilet – it is rarely used, has a nice cold floor to rest your forehead on, and a light that can be switched off
3. If stuck at your desk, disconnect the telephone, prop the silent receiver between ear and shoulder, and lower your tired eyes towards your notepad with pen resting in your hand

children, run the gauntlet of cholera in earthquake zones, visit Wolverhampton and, worst of all, befriend the agents of people who want to go on reality TV.

GETTING TO GRIPS WITH ECCIES

The subject of drink inevitably brings the bluffer to the thorny issue of expenses, which rightly occupies most of a journalist's conscious thought. Hacks are so poorly paid that, traditionally, expenses are regarded the same way a French waiter does his tips – a God-given right they are prepared to kill for, if necessary.

A journalist who has just landed a big story may find their expenses signed off quicker and with fewer slices than usual as a reward. Others who struggle to get a scoop will fail to convince their desk it really was £4.40 for a cup of tea in Leeds.

Managers have found a variety of ways to make submitting a claim slow, painful and ultimately fruitless, including three-month cut-off dates and online forms that you need a degree in further maths to complete.

BLUFFER'S TIP: *News budgets are so tight that many desks receive a bonus for cutting reporters' expenses claims by 10% or so; the canny bluffer therefore inflates them by 20% before submitting.*

However, it is worth persevering. Doing your expenses will earn you the most money per hour at any point in your career. If everyone in a newsroom caught up with their 'eccies', they'd bankrupt the place.

Forging receipts, making up of car journeys and associated barefaced lies are all fraudulent and must never be encouraged in writing. It is common, though, for receipts to be lost and in need of replacement, as well as there to be outlays for which no receipt was possible – such as the purchase of drugs for celebrities who demand recreational pick-me-ups for stories, a hurried taxi chase with no time to hang about, or operations in a foreign country where paperwork is, shall we say, optional.

Expenses used to be a rich training ground for the finest bluffers, in which it was possible to learn from the greats how to wangle another £200 a week out of the Proprietor by dint of just looking busy. These days 21st century technology has brought with it an upsetting habit of computerised receipts complete with bar codes that are impossible to forge.

Foreign travel provides rich pickings with untraceable claims for fixers, corrupt policemen, translators, drivers, camels, camel livery, camel food, or veterinary fees for disposal of camel. Blank books of receipts in the local lingo and currency can be picked up in most supermarkets or post offices. This technique is most successful in countries with different alphabets or complex language, but the wise bluffer first checks that no-one in accounts can speak it.

DO SAY: *"Here's that story you wanted, yes it is rather a zinger isn't it, had to wine and dine a few people for that one, here's the eccies when you have a moment."*

DON'T SAY: *"I completely failed to get a quote. D'you think it would it be all right to get my bus fare back?"*

DEALING WITH HM CONSTABULARY

Once you have learned to survive drink and office politics you must turn your thoughts to how to make it onto the front page without going to jail. As the previous chapter should have made clear, almost any law can be used to stop the most innocent of journalistic tasks.

Keep an up-to-date copy of McNae's Essential Law for Journalists about you at all times – you may never bother to read it, but it can be used as a pillow if your prison cell lacks one. Try not to get locked up, but if you are make sure you write a book about it. Have the newsroom lawyer on speed-dial and remember the correct way to deal with police officers is this:

POLICEMAN: *'Ello, 'ello, what have we here? 'As you been stealin'/conspirin'/terrorisin'/'arassin'/pervertin' public morals?*

JOURNALIST (coolly): *No, officer, I'm carrying out legal and ethical investigations on behalf of (Add Media Outlet Here).*

POLICEMAN (snorting derisively): *Oh ho, I 'ave heard it all now, effical indeed. I believe you are contravening the latest counter-terrorism legislation I learned about in a training session last week and am aching to use on the first villain who crosses my path, which is you matey (reaches for handcuffs).*

JOURNALIST: *That's interesting, Officer… ah, your badge says number 3982, let me just make a note. Could you tell me the precise wording of that clause, the evidential requirements, and how it competes with Article 10 of the Human Rights Act 1998/the Attorney General's latest direction on police misapplying laws to journalists/the*

fact your chief constable is best friends with my editor?
(Adopts honest, inquiring face, pen poised, recorder
on, and hopefully with cameraman or photographer
capturing the moment.)
POLICEMAN: *Oh, er, um, well, just don't do it again*
(proceeds sourly in a northerly direction).

There's no need for you to know what the Attorney
General really said (if anything), or whether The Editor
has the slightest contact with the chief constable. Police
officers know a little about a lot of laws, while journalists
know how to wriggle past those they are battered with
regularly. This is about the bluff, and the most powerful
weapon you have in your armoury is that they all have
a badge number. Make a point of noting it, and they
always back down.

If they persist, call the lawyer and ask them to
discuss your offence with the arresting officer. If you
end up in a cell, remember you get one call and it's
always overheard by the police – ring the lawyer and
tell them where you are and what you are accused of,
confess nothing, and move the problem above your
pay grade. Don't ring the newsdesk or a colleague: you
could be in there for a week before they sober up and
remember you need help.

'The liberty of the press is a blessing when we are inclined to write against others, and a calamity when we find ourselves overborne by the multitude of our assailants.'

Samuel Johnson

KNOCK KNOCK

Other forms of trouble the bluffer may stumble into include war zones (don't be on the wrong side), humanitarian disasters (don't drink the water), riots (don't throw anything) and over-zealous visa officials (act dumb and pray there's no cavity search). But the most danger you will ever be in is knocking on a door.

You may talk to journalists every day; most people only do so when something extreme has happened. A birth, a murder, a lottery win, a coach tragedy. They will be emotional, irrational, and as likely to sob on your shoulder as punch you in the face.

Your first contact may be with a letter, delivered under a door bolted against the Fleet Street scum. They usually go something like this:

"Dear Whoever, This must be an incredibly difficult/sad/exciting time for you, and I know other papers have harassed/offended/offered pitiful sums of money for your story. But if you want the space to defend yourself/ensure the truth is told/pay fitting tribute to (insert name of deceased loved one), please contact me on the number below. I can assure you my editor has expressed sympathy with your plight/wants to campaign on this issue/will pay more than other outlets, and a sensitively-written story will enable you to control what other media report. Please contact me in confidence on XXXXX."

Knocking on a door may be daunting, but it is the easy part. When someone opens it, you must find the right lever to persuade them you're trustworthy in under 20 seconds. Remove sunglasses to make eye contact, remove spectacles so they can't be smashed, and adopt a sympathetic smile even, and sometimes especially, if they're snarling in your face. Use your first name (it helps to humanise you) and be just as polite as you hope a journalist would be if they spoke to your mum.

If someone screams at you for intruding on grief/privacy/personal space, you may wish to mention – if they'll let you – a 2012 study by Liverpool John Moores University which found that bereaved families were prepared by police for media approaches, and felt "let down" when journalists relied solely on social media tributes. Not only can these be inaccurate, but the subsequent headlines come as a shock to relatives still awaiting the 'deathknock'.

The study found "the majority of encounters between journalists and the bereaved are anticipated and positive – particularly in the regions... many of the bereaved wish to actively participate in stories about their loved ones".

background and guided the journalists' inquiries into Richard Nixon's dirty tricks.

BLUFFER'S TIP: *Deep Throat was correctly outed just two years after the scandal broke, as FBI associate director Mark Felt. Woodward and Bernstein denied it for 40 years, and confirmed it only in 2005, when he was suffering from dementia and it was admitted by his family lawyer. It's called "protecting your sources", and more people ought to remember it.*

There is one more interview technique that should be mentioned, but rarely used. It is the nuclear option – silence.

Stare at your target. They feel uncomfortable. Stare more. They say how weird this is. Keep staring. They witter. You raise an eyebrow; the chatter continues. You feign disinterest, and they keep talking until they say something they didn't want to. In effect you have dug a huge pit of silence in front of them, and watched them fall into it. It's a technique used in police interviews, so be aware if it is ever used on you that the only defence is to stare silently back.

BLUFFER'S TIP: *All journalists tend to work for long periods without time off, and are, technically, given days in lieu. Don't ask the desk for one of these. Stamp into the office unwashed from two weeks on the road, throw down a story/gift of foreign biscuits/bloodied bandage and declare loudly; "Well, dysentery was fun". File your expenses, and on your way out of the door tell them you'll be back in next week. They'll be too impressed to argue.*

Doorknocking is dangerous because murderers all have front doors, as do rapists and neo-Nazis. Few of them will appreciate your attentions, and if you're lucky they'll just tell you to f*** off.

It has been known for reporters to be invited in, only for that door to be locked behind them. Journalists can be targeted for their work in Worcester far more easily than a war zone, the difference being that in the Midlands there's no-one looking out for you.

Never knock on a door without the photographer or cameraman nearby and aware of it. If you enter the property alone, remember where the door is. And if the hackles stand up on the back of your neck, trust your instincts and get out.

Remember this gruesome truth: if a policeman is attacked during the course of their job, the miscreant is tracked down, thrown in a cell, and appears before magistrates with a suspicious number of size 10 boot prints on his face. When a journalist is attacked during the course of their job, the suspect tells police they were harassed, the CPS sees no chance of a conviction, and if it does get to court a jury will never believe you.

The most useful weapons you have are pens, cameras, and self-defence classes. Choose one run by an ex-police officer, because they know how to get a rampaging rugby player on the ground without leaving a bruise.

Most doors you knock on just have an ordinary person behind them. Be kind to them, and they'll probably be kind to you.

Survival Checklist

To survive in journalism, you will need to bluff your way onto the front page or top of the bulletins at least once a month. In order to do this, you will need to:

1. Bluff a contact
2. Bluff the authorities
3. Bluff the desk
4. Bluff The Editor
5. Bluff the lawyer
6. Bluff the sub
7. Bluff them all you were drunk at the time
8. Grab a handful of receipts while you're at it

Which is why in journalism the most important skill is the ability to bluff that you are capable of this much bluff.

BROKEN NEWS

Civilians, judges and interns all share the charming fantasy that news is broken by something happening, and someone telling everyone else about it.

As already seen, the thing that happened is rarely told in full, due to pressures of space, interest, law, and spin. What bluffers need to know is that there are four phenomena that have broken the news as we know it.

1. FAKE NEWS

A bluffer will assume a knowing air and point out that fake news was not invented by Donald Trump, much as he might like to claim it was. It's been around as long as humankind – the first time someone painted a picture on the cave wall of the bison they had for lunch, it probably looked bigger than it actually was.

Fake news used to be propaganda, and has been used in every human conflict, most elections, and quite a few seductions. But it has changed. It is no longer a lie told to gain sympathy or power, but to undermine faith in the truth.

So it doesn't matter to Vladimir Putin that his St Petersburg troll factories have been repeatedly exposed by journalists and hackers, who've revealed to the world how false information is disseminated over the internet to promote Russian interests, subvert democracy, and sow discord about trigger issues like immigration.

All he has to do, to further undermine those institutions, is call his fake news operation "fake news" itself. The same goes for Trump – he and his administration put out falsehoods about the size of crowds at his inauguration, and when photographs clearly show them for lies he blamed fake news operatives assigned to make him look 'bad'. Fake news is the spreading of misinformation, and includes lying about your own lies. Journalists the world over struggle with how to combat this, as unwelcome news is increasingly greeted with the sort of bare-faced denial that never used to be believed, but now, frustratingly, is – or at least by enough people to give the myth more traction than the facts.

In 2018 data scientists reported that, of 126,000 rumours spread by 3million people on Twitter between 2006 and 2017, fake news travelled six times further, and faster, than the truth. The top 1% of fake news was seen by between 1,000 and 100,000 people, while the truth rarely got seen by more than 1,000.

The problem was that fake news was more likely to sound 'new' – to be something the reader hadn't seen before. It sparked strong emotions like fear, surprise or disgust. Humans were more likely to share new, shocking falsehoods than the real news, so the more bonkers it is the more likely it is to go viral.

BLUFFER'S TIP: *It will increase the bluffer's chances of being taken for an expert if you can prove that 'old' media is no stranger to fake news. Freddie Starr never really ate a hamster, the Sun did not have 'The Truth' about Hillsborough, and both the Daily Mirror and Sunday Times were famously hoaxed all the way to the front page – the former by faked pictures of soldiers urinating on Iraqi prisoners, and the latter by Adolf Hitler's diaries which were written by a petty criminal.*

Fake news is not a result of technology. It is the normal human business of telling lies for your own ends, and it's enabled by the ignorance and laziness of both the average reader, and the average journalist.

People who get their news from Facebook are victims of an algorithm that shows them only things they agree with. People who do so on Twitter hear only from people they choose to follow. Search engines learn the sort of thing you look for and tailor results according to your past behaviour. Most people don't know this, and don't have the time or inclination to overcome it. As a journalist, it's your job to use multiple sources to verify information, switch between search engines regularly, follow media outlets from all sides of the political spectrum and spot the tell-tale signs of a Photoshopped picture.

Other people regard journalists as a shortcut to the truth. What you write, tweet, share or otherwise publish will be more easily accepted as fact by others – so don't fall into the trap of being first at the expense of being right. Merely re-sharing what someone else wrote does not alleviate you of responsibility, because you are adding journalistic weight to something you haven't checked.

Troll factories are organised liars, but individual trolls are different – socially maladjusted sickos who lurk online to threaten feminists with rape, post abuse on Facebook memorial pages, or pick fights with journalists who are symbols of the Establishment (when they're the most disestablishment people you're likely to meet).

A troll can be easily spotted:

a. No genuine photograph
b. Inclination to fill character count with CAPITAL LETTERS
c. Attempts to create emotional reaction
d. Narcissistic, egotistical, illiterate
e. Probably has a flag, motorbike or numbers in their profile/handle

They can be defeated by remaining calm, never rising to digs, and correcting their spelling and punctuation. Journalists are best at this because trolls are simply the latest incarnation of the Green Ink Brigade – those loyal readers who for centuries wrote letters in green ink to journalists whose articles they disliked. Such letters were always warmly welcomed as evidence someone, at least, had read it. They are less common now, because such writers have mostly taken to Twitter. The correct response is to thank them for reading, advise them to read it again, and suggest a grown-up help with the difficult words.

If accused by someone powerful of producing fake news, even if you produce the proof they'll never admit they were wrong. It does convince readers, though.

After Donald Trump rang Bob Woodward to complain about his latest book, the Washington Post released a tape of their conversation. Publish the transcripts, the documents, the unseen footage that didn't make the edit but can add credibility to your tale. The only way to beat fake news is for those with real news to work harder.

2. BIG DATA

Bluffers will show they're part of the digital zeitgeist if they pronounce that one of the things journalists must be better at in a world filled with new technology is data – the getting, storing, combing through and dissemination thereof.

It would help if, along with shorthand, journalists learned coding because increasingly stories are both hidden and discovered online. How can you find a troll without an expert to trace tweets to their source? Can you find the name and address of who owns a website, or track a virtual transaction? And how do you keep your research for a story safe so that it complies with the Data Protection Act, yet publish it in accordance with the exemption for journalists, when your data storage methods involve writing things on the backs of beer mats?

This is where data journalists come into their own. They are more often whizzkids who have ended up in journalism by accident, as their work requires skills rarely acquired by those who start out using words. The best known examples are the hackers and activists who set up Wikileaks in 2006, and have since sifted through

Which is perhaps why offering to help them pay tribute gets you further than shouting through their letterbox.

GETTING THE STORY

Once inside, your real problems start. You must now interview someone who is highly-emotional and has their guard up. Do not attempt the sort of threatening tactics employed by journalists in TV dramas – it wouldn't work on a two-year-old. Instead remember the mantra: Flirtation, Seduction, Betrayal.

FLIRTATION: Show you like them. Maintain eye contact, open body language, and nod sympathetically at all they say.

SEDUCTION: Connect. Tell them you have experienced similar tragedy. That you were deeply moved by their plight, could persuade the Editor to run a campaign, and their story will produce meaningful change.

BETRAYAL: The act of publishing what you get from the above.

A good bluffer will not only be able to manage an expert interview, they'll be able to go back again next week and do it all over again. In a different context such partnerships can achieve great things. The best example may be Deep Throat (see Glossary), the sometime intelligence contact and "incurable gossip" contacted by Bob Woodward at the start of Watergate. After the pair established trust, they met repeatedly for years, often in an underground car park, as the source provided deep and made public more than 10 million documents. They have published Iraq war logs revealing 15,000 deaths that were previously unknown, video footage of US forces targeting Iraqi journalists, and US diplomatic cables that revealed, among other not-shocking things, that Prince Andrew was a buffoon, Silvio Berlusconi was vain and the Chinese had hacked the Dalai Lama. They were condemned worldwide, not least because they failed to redact social security numbers, suicide attempts, and other sensitive information. Wikileaks was recently subject of a leak themselves, which they did not appear to enjoy but everyone else did.

DO SAY: *'Wikileaks has been suspiciously quiet about the Russians, don't you think?'*
DON'T SAY: *'What's encryption when it's at home?'*

Never attempt to bluff anyone you are a 'data journalist' unless you speak AWK. Instead concentrate on charming those who understand this stuff, and persuade them you can get their hard work into the mainstream.

Occasionally you will have no choice but to wade through vast swathes of data yourself. A prime example of this was the 2008 Parliamentary expenses scandal, when a series of FOI battles compelled MPs and peers to release their dodgy claims. The authorities insisted on redacting the names, but one of those doing the redaction sold the uncensored data to the Daily Telegraph.

A squad of reporters locked in a side office and operating in total secrecy had to comb through years of claims from 800 peers and 650 MPs, cross-referencing with other sources to expose those who gamed the system to pay for homes, nannies, duck houses, moats and tennis court repairs. It was a monster job, and unlikely to be repeated – other newspapers had already turned the story down.

It is more common with big leaks to find news outlets co-operating, because there's so much data to deal with. This happened with the Wikileaks "Cablegate" story, with one reputable outlet chosen in a dozen different countries to ensure worldwide coverage. Something similar happened with the "Panama Papers" – an anonymous leak of 11.5million documents about more than 214,000 clients of Panamanian law firm Mossack Fonseca. Bluffers don't need to know the finer details of either: it is enough to hint that you have stored it all in your own organic memory bank, currently encrypted in a language known only to yourself.

DO SAY: *'At 2.6 terabytes, the Panama Papers were 1,500 times bigger than Wikileaks' Cablegate.'*
DON'T SAY: *'I think I've deleted it.'*

3. ANTI-SOCIAL MEDIA

As technology has changed society, so the media has had to adapt to keep up. Journalists need to know how to search a database and exploit an algorithm, and also why they might not want *everything* they do to be electronically recorded.

Social media is increasingly used to break news – as well as to find it.

If old hands complain about the internet mucking up the true business of journalism, bluffers should point out that it is no more than a way of organising human misbehaviour, and all that's changed over the centuries is that shenanigans are now searchable. It makes the business of exposure quicker, and more legally-sound, even if it is a lot less enjoyable than drinking the Prince of Wales' old school friends under the table and picking their memories when they can't fight back.

DO SAY: *'I saw a highly-localised trend and am deep-mining the algorithm to scrape the best content.'*
DON'T SAY: *'Nah, I'm just pissing about on Twitter.'*

4. PUBLIC OUTRAGE

The fourth and final way that news is broken – regularly, it seems – is that journalists just can't help themselves.

The media has been the subject of its own scandals ever since the invention of movable type. Hugh Grant may want a final solution that would stop journalists committing crimes and misdemeanours, but in the absence of anyone finding how to reprogramme the human genome to comply with his wishes it's highly unlikely.

Journalists object to authority. It doesn't matter whose, anyone's will do. They flout the will of The Editor at their peril, but news desks, proprietors, accounts departments, lawyers, local authorities and most public bodies and corporations have all had occasion to fling their hands up and demand of the heavens why that reporter won't take piss off for an answer.

Some journalists are so good at this that even when the story turns out to not be true, they won't believe it if told by someone in authority. They have invested so much time and effort, and find it so easy to believe the story they've heard is the truth, that they won't let go of it even if everything looks wrong.

Such pig-headedness leads to mistakes, and when they are capable of convincing others, their mistakes are sometimes spotted only after publication.

Journalists, despite all appearances to the contrary, are credulous souls. They want to believe, and – in the same way fake news tickles the toes of everyone on social media – the more outlandish a claim may be, the keener they are to prove it.

The same applies to information that's hard to get. If I can access a prince's voicemail, why shouldn't I? The little beggar would never admit it if you just asked him. The thirst to be right, to be first, to get your name on a scandal with the suffix '-gate', is too strong a temptation for most hacks to withstand.

Thus they get drawn into misbehaviour that causes problems for the rest of the Fourth Estate.

DO SAY: *'Sometimes the best story is the one you're not named in.'*

DON'T SAY: *'This would be so much easier if we could get into the police files like the good old days.'*

When popular TV host Russell Harty was dying in hospital of hepatitis in 1988, the Sun and the Sunday Mirror published long-whispered rumours of his homosexuality and a possible link to the dreaded AIDS virus. It was a cruel time to out someone, deeply unwise to do it to a national treasure, and led to playwright Alan Bennett thundering in the funeral eulogy: "The gutter press finished him off."

Two years later when 'Allo 'Allo star Gorden Kaye was recovering in hospital from emergency brain surgery following a road accident, a reporter and photographer from the Sunday Sport walked into his room, conducted an interview and splashed a picture of him in his hospital bed. He was not only well-loved, but incredibly vulnerable – friends were playing him videos of his acting to remind him who he was. Kaye sued, but the court ruled there was no remedy in English law for an invasion of privacy.

These and other cock-ups led to the dissolution of the inept Press Council and formation of the Press Complaints Commission (PCC), along with a code of conduct which expressly forbade such invasions of privacy, as well as pejorative references to sexuality or clandestine entry into hospitals.

It was enough, for a bit. The News of the World was compelled to print a full-page, 36-point PCC ruling on its handling of a story about the death of a former boyfriend of Labour MP Clare Short. But it is impossible to put a permanent lid on the Press, not just because they are naturally bumptious but because you can't put a lid on the news.

So when Andrew Morton's book on Princess Diana revealed bulimia, suicide attempts and the true state of her marriage to Charles, there was a feeding frenzy. PCC chairman Lord MacGregor publicly condemned "the odious exhibition of journalists dabbing their fingers in the stuff of other people's souls", only for it to be discovered within days that Diana had co-operated with the book.

Then the Sunday People reported that Tory minister David Mellor, who said the Press was "drinking in the last chance saloon" before state regulation, had cavorted with the actress Antonia de Sancha while wearing the top half of a Chelsea football strip. There were reports, later denied, of toe-sucking, soon matched by long-lens photographs of the Duchess of York indulging in the same fetish with her financial adviser.

At the end of 1993 the Sunday Mirror published secret pictures of Diana working out in the gym, and Lord MacGregor – quite extraordinarily – called for an advertisers' boycott. The Mirror Group pulled out of the PCC in a huff and self-regulation was in crisis, until the main publishers sat down to stitch together a compromise.

Most of the 90s and Noughties were well-behaved, perhaps because many of those involved in earlier misdemeanours had been promoted, demoted or retired. There were a few thousand complaints every year, most adjudicated to the complainants' satisfaction. The system seemed to work.

But the Press did what it always does, and pushed it. In 2009 there were 25,000 complaints to the PCC, most of them about an article written by Jan Moir in the Daily Mail claiming that Boyzone singer Stephen Gateley's sudden death was "sleazy" and linked to his "gay lifestyle". In fact, he had an undiagnosed heart condition. The PCC did not uphold the complaints, considering the article tasteless but an example of free expression.

In the same year a number of tabloid journalists were subject to a sting, and recorded on undercover cameras discussing obtaining celebrities' medical information and how little regard they had for the PCC. In 2011 Northern & Shell, which owned the Express group, pulled out of the regulator in a hissy fit about the number of expensive complaints it was getting. The final, fatal blow was struck with the phone-hacking scandal, which swallowed the floundering PCC for good.

HACKED-OFF

At some stage during their mastery of journalism, bluffers will be expected to demonstrate a coherent and well argued case about the phone-hacking scandal. The main thing you need to know is that it didn't go well for anyone, a handful of people were arrested, and the most successful English-language newspaper in the world closed with the loss of hundreds of jobs.

It took six years to be exposed. What began in 2005 as revelations about listening to the voicemails of celebrities and politicians grew to encompass first 'Diana's beloved boys' and then, appallingly, a murdered schoolgirl.

OMNISHAMBLES

Milly Dowler was 13 when she went missing in March 2002, and it was 6 months before her body was found. In between was a long summer of stories involving tearful appeals by her family, a £100,000 reward for information from the Sun, and a catalogue of police blunders. Officers first decided she'd run away, then that she was dead, then that she'd been done away with by someone she knew and lastly that her innocent father was responsible. Amid this madness, News of the World (NOTW) chief reporter Neville Thurlbeck commissioned Glenn Mulcaire (see also pages 57–58) to investigate.

Thurlbeck told subsequent court hearings that Mulcaire claimed a 'police contact' had told him about voicemails on Milly's phone. The messages – later found to be the result of a wrong number – were about a job at a factory in Telford, and gave the impression Milly was alive and seeking work. Half a dozen journalists were despatched to the factory, and when no sign of Milly was found Surrey Police were contacted. Executives told coppers they'd heard the voicemails. A story about the 'hoax messages' on Milly's phone later appeared in the paper.

In the years after Milly's body was discovered there were repeated stories about police's failure to find her killer. Several people were jailed for harassing police and her family, some claiming responsibility and others claiming to be Milly herself.

In the meantime, phone-hacking became public knowledge. The two princes sought police help over their missing messages, Clive Goodman was jailed along with Mulcaire, and a treasure trove of notebooks provided evidence that Mulcaire had hacked the phones of dozens of celebrities.

MORE PUBLIC OUTRAGE

The PCC held inquiries into the issue in 2007 and 2009. It believed Goodman was a "rogue" reporter, failed to question anyone other than his editor, and reported that it had not been misled when, er, it had.

At first the issue was little more than public titillation about celebrity secrets and journalistic sneakiness, none of which was surprising. Former editor Andy Coulson, once Goodman's boss, had moved into Downing Street as the spin doctor for David Cameron, and both the Left-wing Guardian and Labour politicians wanted to take him down.

But at the end of June 2011 serial killer Levi Bellfield – linked to Milly after almost a decade of police cock-ups – was finally convicted of her murder. Just 11 days later the Guardian splashed on a leak from the police hacking investigation that the NOTW had listened to her voicemails. Worse, they had intentionally deleted messages to free space for her to leave more, thereby giving her family 'false hope' she was alive.

The outrage was immediate, and immense. Social media campaigns led to an advertisers' boycott, editor Rebekah Wade was reviled as a witch, Coulson was arrested, and the News of the World closed six days later. The PCC went the same way within a few months, finally accepting its own irrelevance.

JACK-KNIFED

Politicians led by Labour MP Tom Watson did what the PCC hadn't, and hauled those concerned in for questioning by the media select committee. They campaigned for and got a judge-led inquiry, where Milly's parents relived the moment when they realised a message had been deleted and said: "She's alive!" The print media was publicly disemboweled, and their broadcast brethren livestreamed it.

Journalists were terrified, many arrested, but only a handful jailed. Coulson, the biggest scalp, served 5 months of an 18-month sentence for conspiracy to illegally intercept communications. Thurlbeck served just 37 days, claiming he was trying to find a girl who he thought was alive. Watson was elected to the deputy leadership of his party. Celebrities got millions in damages. The politicians who ordered the inquiry conspicuously failed to hold the second part, about the relationships between politicians and the Press. Guardian reporters were questioned over similar use of police leaks and phone-hacking, but were not charged. Perhaps they were not the prey, and perhaps it was because they had, as Harold Evans advised, put it in their copy.

The truth finally surfaced in December 2011, when the Met admitted it was "unlikely" the NOTW had deleted messages, as they were also listened to by police, and were in any case automatically removed by the phone provider after a set period. The horrific 'false hope' moment was nobody's fault.

Despite calling for prominent and prompt corrections by others, the Guardian carried the Met's revelation on page 10, corrected the online version only 3 days later, and put the correction in a footnote. The strap and headline, at time of writing, still give the impression that hacks let the parents of a murdered girl believe she was alive.

Phone-hacking was a scandal that nobody benefitted from. Milly's family were grossly failed by police, celebrity gossip didn't lose popularity, politicians proved themselves hypocrites again, and journalism itself jackknifed on the actions of those – tabloid and broadsheet - who thought they were better than everyone else.

ENTER IPSO

This time there wasn't just talk of state regulation. An ombudsman was set up and regulated by a Royal Charter, which was itself approved by the Privy Council consisting of current and former politicians, judges, and peers.

Parliament passed the Crime and Courts Act 2013 which made papers that failed to recognise the new regulator liable for costs if they were sued, even if they won. Newspapers were furious, and this time even those who had criticised their excesses backed them. The Guardian and FT refused to join the new regulator, along with Private Eye. Instead newspapers once again set up and funded a successor to the PCC, the Independent Press Standards Organisation, which has so far proved toothsome – forcing its adjudications onto front pages of the Times, Mail and Express, as well as local papers.

At time of writing IPSO is the regulator for 1,500 newspapers and 1,100 websites. Its state-approved opponent, IMPRESS, is the go-to ombudsman for less than 100 small titles, including the Hastings Online Times, Isle of Wight Observer and Iraq Business News. Critics noted it made no criticism of The Canary when it grossly breached suicide reporting guidelines. IMPRESS also ruled against three of its own staff when they broke impartiality rules by tweeting unflattering remarks about the Mail and Sun.

To sum up: journalists are their own worst enemy, and always will be. Bad journalism has only ever been exposed or improved by good journalism. Which is perhaps why the best people to investigate, expose, and regulate journalists are… other journalists.

DO SAY: *'I've always abided by the Editors' Code of Practice, which is open to public consultation unlike the Privy Council which is just a bunch of *****.'*
DON'T SAY: *'Accuracy, schmaccuracy.'*

Once you've bluffed your way in and around journalism, you'll need to tackle the many-headed hydra of fake news, battle with big data, surf through social media and avoid the attentions of your fellow journalists who will mostly be hellbent on destroying either you or themselves.

It will therefore come as no surprise to learn any bluffer with their wits about them needs a final trick up their sleeve – the ability to get out of journalism alive.

BLUFF YOUR WAY OUT

Escape. Run. Hide. Do whatever you can – public relations, if necessary.

Journalism is a tough and thankless job, and a glance around any newsroom will not reveal many happy 90-year-old hacks. Those who look elderly and infirm are probably not much over 40.

There comes a point where most journalists must choose between journalism and normality, between being able to recognise your children and wondering who that small person you tripped over was when you staggered in the door after two weeks covering a mass shooting in Cumbria.

BLUFFER'S TIP: *Never marry a journalist. They know exactly what you get up to, and if they don't, they know how to find out.*

It's not an impossible task to leave the newsroom behind. All the skills you learned will stand you in excellent stead for any one of a number of future, more lucrative and less soul-consuming careers:

1. FREELANCE LIFE, AKA THE BEST OF BOTH WORLDS

The preferred option of those addicted to typing and who did their best work in a different time zone. It will require good contacts, a constant stream of commissions, and a redundancy cheque as a cushion. Say so long to corporate emails, oppressive supervision, and paid holidays.

It will take 6 months to depressurize and three months, on average, to get paid – that's if they haven't eaten your invoice. But there will come a day when a former boss says 'thanks' and your battered, ink-stained soul will begin to recover. You might even get a gig as a columnist if you're really lucky.

You also get to work in your pyjamas and knock off at 3pm.

2. PUBLIC RELATIONS, AKA THE DARK SIDE

A common emergency exit for journalists, who know from experience that hospitals, police forces, celebrities and government departments are in dire need of help. Good journalists opt for the shorter hours and greater pay, and will swiftly gravitate to management positions. Poor journalists opt for the quiet life, and will sink to ringing hacks on deadline asking if they received the press release they spiked three days earlier.

It's easy to bluff your way in this job – you simply need to be a plausible prevaricator and selectively deaf. Hacks will forever deride you as 'the headlice of civilisation', as the journalist AA Gill described PRs. Who cares – there's a pension, long lunches, and inferiors to bring you coffee.

3. GOVERNMENT ADVISER

Similar to the above, but rather than explaining to journalists how they got the story wrong you explain to those in power how to tell a different story. Highly-paid, grossly unethical, and a common finishing school for privately-educated political hacks who got themselves into power without having to get elected first.

4. CRISIS COMMS CONSULTANCY

Your clients have journalists on their doorstep asking uncomfortable questions about their offshore funds, relationship status or once-private fetish. Your job is to find a way through the minefield. You may brief friendly journalists, smuggle clients out of the country, or train them to face down John Humphrys without crying. You will earn big money, and in an ideal world will be paid monthly retainers by showbiz and corporate clients. But your phone will never be off and you'll eat, sleep and breathe the news cycle.

5. DEBT COLLECTOR

After a year or two of journalism you can find anyone, anywhere, and put the wind up them twice before tea-time. You'll also be good at ducking.

6. CRIME LORD

See above, add an ability to falsify records, manipulate loyalties and manoeuvre yourself out of trouble while tiptoeing around the legal niceties. Successful crime, like journalism, requires a strong work ethic and survival skills.

7. ACADEMIA

A gentle backwater for journalists who like telling war stories to pop-eyed undergraduates. They may question whether you really did liberate Mogadishu single-handed before the UN got there, and what use it would be to them in their likely future career of copying celebrity captions off Instagram. There are long holidays and the students probably won't call you the same names The Editor did.

8. SALES AND MARKETING

The last resort of the truly desperate, in which you will attempt to use your ability to sell a story to a bored editor to persuade half-asleep people to buy a product they don't need.

Pay not great, even less than journalism, but at least you can tell people what you do at parties and they won't sneer.

A QUESTION OF BALANCE

Journalism is all about balance between the half of your brain that is a hack and the half that is a normal human. You may hate doing deathknocks, resent being reviled, and object to standing up to your knees in the rotting corpses of people you've never been introduced to. But at the same time you're thinking 'this is a BRILLIANT story, it writes like butter, it's a definite splash, probably going to change the world and I bet I get an award for this...' The trick is to walk the tightrope between the two states. If you wobble too far in one direction you lose the steel you need to be able to knock on someone's door and ruin their day. If you go too far the other way, you become the kind of person who hacks a dead schoolgirl's voicemails without a qualm.

If you can't hold the line between the two, you are failing The Reader, failing at journalism in general, and failing to maintain your bluff. You must escape before your bluff is discovered.

But first there's one thing all journalists want when they finally leave the newsroom behind. They want to be **banged out.**

BANGING OUT

It may sound crude, but like the final item on the news list it's mawkishly sentimental. It refers to the days of hot metal, when a printer retired, and his colleagues would reach for the nearest metal object – usually the tray the type was arranged in – and bang it upon their metal composing 'stone'. Echoing off the huge metal presses, it produced a shattering sound in Fleet Street's basements.

Printing has been reduced to a few ink-stained technicians a long way from the newsroom, but journalists have kept the tradition alive. Those accepted as one will find when they depart the office for the last time their colleagues reach for the nearest object – stapler, computer mouse, enemy skull – and bang it on the desk.

There are two things to look out for. The first is that, however many people may start at different times, the banging finds its own rhythm. Within a few strikes the whole newsroom is synchronised, proving co-ordinated journalism can shake the world.

The second is that if you are banged out, it means you have won the approval of journalists, which is probably the hardest thing for any human being to do.

Being banged out is proof that you bluffed the world's finest bluffers, and lived to tell the tale.

MORE FOLLOWS LATER

(see Glossary under MFL)

It doesn't matter what journalism you do or how long you do it for, the question screaming at the heart of every hack's soul is: 'What next?'

Journalism has barely changed in its fundamentals since the invention of printing. It is the collection of gossip and information, organising it, and passing it on to others in a way they'll want to pay for. Now, as in 1702, there are many who disapprove, think it low-rent hackery, and yet crave journalistic approval.

The world has more readers and more hacks than at any point in human history. Yet it is harder than ever to make people pay for it. A paper boy could once wave a copy of the *Daily Courant* aloft, shouting its headlines about the battles of foreign wars, and customers paid for something they could hold in their hand. Today news is in the air, fast, and hard to grasp. People don't hold onto, or value, it much at all.

Profits have dipped in spite of the fact there are more readers. The problem, it now appears, lies with those things the *Daily Courant* had on the back page and relied on for its editorial independence – adverts.

NECESSARY EVIL

While readers often complain that there are too many adverts, without them we would all be reduced to hearing only the news rich men wanted us told. Imagine a world where pension funds and investment managers set the news agenda and ask yourself if you want that. Journalists at least report on each other's misdeeds sometimes; bankers not so much.

Yet advertisers pay less per reader online than they did in print, for more intimate and provable access. Across the European Union as a whole, newspaper ad revenues fell from 22 billion Euros in 2009 to 15.7 billion in 2015. The same pattern is now emerging in TV as advertising moves online with the audience.

Internet ads do not have the same return on investment, can be blocked, unnoticed, or cause older computers to crash and burn. Reader surveys, subscription offers and tricks to increase engagement all help, but don't hold attention. But there is still all to play for.

NEWS ON DEMAND

There are ways around this. News outlets could act as one, and put up paywalls simultaneously. Perhaps even a system where if you pay to access one you can access them all (Imagine! Sun readers flicking through the Guardian!). But there would never be enough resources to legally pursue the treacherous bloggers who copy and paste great swathes of text.

Or the world could – by consensus or gravity – move towards a system of news aggregation, with customers buying news as simply as they buy music on iTunes. One site has your login details, all outlets upload their stories, and you can browse or subscribe to effectively 'build' your own paper, with news from the Times, features from the Mirror, or sport from the BBC. A few people have had ideas in this direction already, with limited success.

Maybe the answer is to decide that news, on principle, MUST be free and not shut off to those who aren't online, endure rural broadband or won't let PayPal through their tinfoil hat. Free newspapers do fairly well – the DMG-owned Metro has a 1.4m circulation and is read by three times that number when it's left on trains and buses every day. It makes money, yet it's not the must-read it could be with investment.

But if journalism was free, who would value it? We tend to treasure only what is hard to get.

CRITICAL TIMES

At the same time journalism has never had as many enemies. There's fake news, over-baked news, showbiz spin and secrecy masquerading as privacy. Scandals go untold, data is restricted. The horrors of phone-hacking will occupy current journalists' nightmares for years to come, but those with short or zero memories will push their luck again. With faster news cycles and public outrage turbo-powered by social media, state regulation could once again rear its thoughtless head.

If the stormtroopers of censorship patrol a virtual Fleet Street, there'd soon be a thriving market for journalism in the back streets of the internet. The price you'd pay, as with anything purchased in an alleyway, is confidence in the ingredients. Or maybe we should all just be more French. One recent survey found that 64% of *les Francaises* had no intention of letting go of their newspapers any time soon. Vive le journalisme! Vinyl made a comeback, so why not paper? Yet accounting giant PWC reckons print industry revenues will drop an average of 3% over the five years before 2020 – with digital income rising 10% in the same period. Print is in decline across the developed world, but readership is growing in poorer nations. In richer ones they haven't abandoned journalism, just changed how they get it – in 1995, Germany had 5 newspaper websites. Today there are more than 700.

Whatever way is found, it will be found. Not because journalists are any good at numbers, but because business is very good at finding a way to get money out of people. And most people on the planet read journalism daily.

In 2015 the World Press Trends database estimated there were 3.5bn newspaper readers worldwide, out of a human population of 7.3bn. Almost a billion of them were consuming newspapers online. If you went back in time and told Elizabeth Mallet where the *Daily Courant* would lead, she'd never have sold. And if you told King Charles II, he wouldn't bother with censorship. He'd get himself a website, and a paywall.

Meanwhile, journalism will continue to break stories, irritate the powerful and entertain The Reader. More scandals about journalists themselves are inevitable, along with politicians calling for a crackdown, being caught with their pants down, and demanding a proper privacy law – to protect others, of course.

Journalists will always push back, because they don't know how to do anything else. To overcome all these hurdles you will need:

1. An official-looking lanyard
2. A hi-vis jacket
3. A pen

The first two can bluff you past any security in the world. The third really is mightier than the sword – not just in the power of whatever it is used to write, but because it can also be jammed in an assailant's ear to enable a quick getaway.

Get a driving licence. Use the spell check. Keep the receipts. Remember that Fleet Street isn't a place so much as a way of life. One that gives you an ability, not just to bluff better than anyone else on the planet, but to triangulate and overcome someone else's bluff even when you're 'tired and emotional'.

Journalism will always be a badly-paid, exciting, dangerous job full of people so deranged they refuse to walk away from fights, whether it's with countries, cartels or Coronation Street has-beens. Sometimes they will save the world, and sometimes the world will have to save them.

It will also, always, be the most fun you can have while typing.

ß

There's no point in pretending that you know everything about journalism – nobody does – but if you've got this far and absorbed at least a modicum of the information and advice contained within these pages, then you will almost certainly know more than 99% of the rest of the human race about what journalism is, how it developed, what it aims to achieve, whether it is a force for good or evil, and why everybody working in it wonders every day whether they've still got a job.

What you now do with this information is up to you, but here's a suggestion: be confident about your newfound knowledge, see how far it takes you, but above all have fun using it. You are now a bona fide expert in the art of bluffing about a subject which will occupy your every waking hour (because stories don't just happen between nine and five).

And remember: one day, who knows, you might actually get to change the world.

GLOSSARY

Algorithm   The online equivalent of whether a newsagent puts your journalism on the top shelf, bottom shelf, or under the counter

Babysitting   Looking after the subject of a story, usually in a hotel, so they don't speak to rivals

Bandwidth   Online equivalent of readers losing their spectacles

Banging out   Winning at life

Breaking news   What Donald Trump does to retain power

Broadsheet press   Unpopular papers with slightly more-popular journalists

Byline   The name on top of a story, occasionally indicating the person who actually wrote it

Churnalism   When press releases replace proper news

Composing stone   The metal printer's bench, upon which he hammered or 'set' the type into frames

Contact   Someone who'll admit they know you

Contempt   What a judge will hold you in if you prejudice a court case

Crosshead   Sub-heading used to break up blocks of copy

Deathknock Asking someone to talk about a dead loved one

Desk The people who hate you most

Doorknock Asking to talk to anyone about anything

Doorstep Sitting outside a house until someone agrees to talk

Deep Throat i) A 1972 porn film about a woman looking for an orgasm, and ii) an unnameable source in the heart of things

Diary story Something everyone knew was happening today, such as a court hearing, town carnival or council meeting

DSMA notice An indication your story is true but the government would prefer if you didn't tell anyone

Ends To be put at the end of copy to indicate the story's over, your phone's off, and you're in the pub

Gutter press Popular papers with unpopular journalists

Heart-starter First alcoholic drink of the day

Herogram An email of praise from The Editor. Rarer than hens' teeth

Hot metal Lost art of printing newspapers using letters cast in lead

Kill fee Paying a freelance not to publish their story

Lower case Hot metal phrase referring to small letters used more often and kept in a lower drawer

Masthead Title of a newspaper or magazine on the front page

MFL More follows later, to be put at the end of copy to indicate there'll be further additions

Moveable type Ability to build any page from a number of moveable elements

NIB News in brief, or story told in two parts or less

Non-attributable Quotable, but without names

Off-diary A story you found yourself

Off-the-record Not to be quoted at all

Off-stone The newspaper has gone to print and it's too late to change it now

Prejudicial If you quote it you might end up before a judge

Pull quote Words extracted from copy and used to draw attention

Secret squirrel Someone you're not supposed to know

Scoop When you beat competitors to a story

Scooped When they beat you

Silver salver Metaphorical means by which a splash is carried to a journalist favoured by their superiors, and despised by everyone else

Source Someone who'll never admit they know you

Spike Vicious office equipment used as a home for old press releases, unused copy, and enemy eyeballs

Splash Main front page story

Splash and a spread Story which runs on the front page as well as two pages inside

Strap Nothing to do with punishment, but a subhead under the main headline in a newspaper or magazine article.

Sub judice Judicial restraint used to threaten journalists not to report a thing they probably should

Tired and emotional Journalistic euphemism for drunk

The Editor Person who thinks they're your boss

The Reader Your actual boss

Upper case Hot metal letters used less often and kept in upper drawer

A BIT MORE BLUFFING...

Available from all good bookshops

bluffers.com